POWER GRAPHICS PRESENTATIONS USING YOUR COMPUTER

POWER GRAPHICS PRESENTATIONS USING YOUR COMPUTER

James Edward Keogh

Macmillan Publishing Company
New York
Collier Macmillan Publishers
London

Copyright © 1985 by James Edward Keogh

All rights reserved. No part of this book may be reproduced or transmitted in any form or by any means, electronic or mechanical, including photocopying, recording or by any information storage and retrieval system, without permission in writing from the Publisher.

Macmillan Publishing Company
866 Third Avenue, New York, N.Y. 10022
Collier Macmillan Canada, Inc.

Library of Congress Cataloging-in-Publication Data
Keogh, James Edward, 1948–
    Power graphics presentations using your computer.
    Includes index.
    1. Computer graphics.   2. Communication in management.
I. Title.
T385.K44   1985   006.6   85-13894
ISBN 0-02-562020-7

Macmillan books are available at special discounts
for bulk purchases for sales promotions, premiums,
fund-raising, or educational use. For details, contact:
    Special Sales Director
    Macmillan Publishing Company
    866 Third Avenue
    New York, N.Y. 10022

10 9 8 7 6 5 4 3 2 1

Printed in the United States of America

Contents

Preface

IN TODAY'S highly competitive business world the most successful presentations, whether targeted for large or small audiences, are the product of many hours of careful preparation. The most persuasive, creative presentations are the work of executives who have learned to combine successfully their hard-earned technical expertise with an indispensable array of up-to-date communication skills.

When a heads-up executive sets out to design and present a corporate strategy, every single step—no matter how small—is put through an exhaustive process of analysis and review. Each word in every document is scrutinized to assure that crucial ideas are properly communicated. Unfortunately, concern for detail cannot be taught; it is the mark of a born winner.

In this book we will examine the proven communication techniques that professional speakers employ to design power-packed presentations and the latest personal computer technology to help you develop your own high-tech presentation style. With a little effort any ambitious executive can adopt these methods. Positive application of these techniques will result in distinctive, effective presentations and enhanced professional status.

Naturally, a key element of any presentation is the set of tools available to you for preparing the handouts, speeches, slides, and other material traditionally part of a professional presentation. One of the most important of these tools is the personal computer.

Power Graphics Presentations Using Your Computer will show you which software to use in conjunction with your personal computer to create dramatic presentation material. Throughout these pages you will find detailed looks at how popular software such as Lotus 1-2-3, Symphony, Framework, and PFS:Write, File, and Graph, among others, can be used as presentation tools.

With the right software your personal computer can also generate high-quality slides that will change a staid, traditional presentation into one that drives home your point. This book shows you how ExecuVision, The Grafix Partner, Peachtree Business Graphics, and other well-tested software packages can be used to produce and enhance your graphic illustrations. Software such as The Grafix Partner can be used in combination with Lotus 1-2-3 and similar programs to produce a dramatic visual effect.

While many of the computer books on the market suggest which software to purchase, you will find that this book gives you valuable step-by-step drive-throughs of some of the more important software packages.

Producing a colorful image on the computer monitor is fine, but how do you transfer this image into material that you can use in a slide presentation? We have included chapters that are specifically designed to show you how to transform the image on your computer screen into overhead transparencies, standard 35-mm slides, and printed illustrations.

Power Graphics Presentations covers both proven techniques that are commonly used in this process and detailed discussions of the equipment that makes these techniques possible. You will find informative discussions on computer monitors, dot matrix printers, ink jet printers, laser printers, thermal-transfer printers, 35-mm cameras, and special monitor cameras that are designed to photograph images from a computer screen. The names and addresses of firms that manufacture this equipment are included for quick reference.

Power Graphics Presentations also gets you thinking creatively about the illustrations used in the presentation. There are detailed discussions about the techniques of presentations, the software needed to generate illustrations, and the equipment that is necessary to produce hard copies of the screen. We have also included a special chapter designed to give the executive ideas for those illustrations. There are over 40 very creative illustrations that were designed using the software discussed in this book. You can quickly look through this gallery to get ideas for your own presentation.

Throughout *Power Graphics Presentations* the emphasis has been placed on creating a professional presentation. Fac-

tors relating to software and equipment that are not specifically applicable to business presentations are not discussed.
Our approach concentrates on giving you a straightforward
and practical guide to creating your own professional presentations.

Meetings, Perceptions, and Presentations

A PICTURE IS worth a thousand words to the innovative executive, and a computer-generated picture can be worth even more! Your personal computer can add an exciting new dimension to your next presentation by producing highly attractive and dramatic art—art that gets your message across. With modern presentation graphics software, your personal computer and printer or plotter can give you the sizzle that scores points with your audience. A unique experience awaits you the first time you create your own presentation art and find that it looks like a professional graphic artist drew it.

Increasingly, smart business executives are turning to in-house, personal computer-generated graphics to illustrate their reports and small group presentations. Imagine the visual impact when your associates, seated before a color monitor, see a sixteen-color animated display of how well regional offices are achieving their goals. Best of all, this capability has a one-time cost of less than $5000.

The heart of the computer-generated illustration is the presentation graphics software package. Presentation graphics software packages are not all the same. Some offer complex graphics capabilities, like animation. Others are limited to simple displays that transfer sets of data into a bar chart. The more versatile the package, the more you can expect to pay for it.

Mid-priced ($100) presentation graphics packages produce simple illustrations, including graphs, bar charts, pie charts, line graphs, scatter diagrams, and tables. These are the minimum features you can expect from the software you purchase.

Expensive software will allow you to produce more complex images. Using these advanced packages you will be able to produce a complete chart with titles and symbols. You'll be able to create spiraling images and other special effects. With some software you can even overlay color graphs one on top of the other to produce a multicolor graph. You will also be able to do animation and dissolve from one display to another.

Before you rush out to buy the latest thing in presentation graphics packages, you should first decide exactly what you need. What are your objectives in purchasing the graphics package? It would be uneconomical to spend hundreds of dollars on a package that features complicated special effects when you can get everything you need in a less expensive program.

Meetings, Meetings, Meetings

We all know that meetings are an integral part of business life. Isn't it odd, then, that so many of these valuable opportunities end up a waste of time? Whether a business meeting is a success depends on a number of factors, some of which are listed below:

- A complete, clear agenda for the meeting is distributed well in advance to everyone who attends.
- Everyone who should be attending the meeting is there on time, prepared to participate.
- Important information is made available to the group, quickly and efficiently, to avoid distractions that disrupt the meeting.
- Everyone follows through on the conclusions reached during the meeting. People don't just go off in their own direction until the next meeting is called.

With a little imagination you can use your personal computer to make meetings work.

An agenda, for example, can be written with a word processing program on your personal computer. In the weeks before the meeting you can type the points you intend to discuss into the personal computer. These notes are saved to a file on a floppy disk and updated periodically as additional thoughts come to mind. A few days before the meeting you or your assistant can tighten up the notes. The items for discussion should be ranked in the order of their importance, so that the least important items can be omitted if the meeting has to be cut short. Once the notes are in a presentable form, have them printed, copied, and distributed to everyone who will be attending the meeting.

Colleagues at distant branch offices cannot be physically brought to the meeting by your personal computer, but your computer can bring the meeting to them. Through the use of a modem (the device that links the personal computer with the telephone) the entire meeting can be held using a computer conferencing system. Each participant can connect his or her computer to a remote conferencing network. The entire discussion is then held by typing questions, answers, and comments into the computer. The computer conferencing system then distributes the text to all the participants. Although associates may be unable to be with you, modems provide a simple way a personal computer can bring employees together.

Making important information available during a meeting can be frustrating. Computers can help you by allowing you to record all potentially necessary information on a floppy disk or having it stored on a mini- or mainframe computer. Again, using a modem and a personal computer (assuming that you have established the proper links with the database), any information that might be called for can be accessed from the conference room right during the meeting. With the data from this remote source feeding into the proper presentation software package, the information can quickly be presented to the group in a pleasant and effective format.

Interruptions during the conference can be reduced by having your personal computer handy. Typically, distractions are caused when participants must leave the conference room to gather additional information. This can be all but eliminated by calling for the information with your personal computer.

In many cases you can improve your meetings simply by guaranteeing that everyone present follow through on the conclusions reached in conference. Again, you can put your personal computer to work to assure an effective follow-up. For example, during the meeting the executive in charge of the group can hand out assignments to the participants and make notes and comments using a personal computer. These assignments are stored on a floppy disk and can be worked up later in a presentable format and printed and distributed to the staff the following day as a reminder of their assignments.

Good meetings, then, don't just happen; you have to make them. They require a planned agenda and careful coordination of activities so that all participants understand their roles in the conference. Nothing will bring a meeting to a screeching halt more quickly than the absence of important information. There is no better high-tech tool for preparing and storing these facts and figures than a personal computer.

COMPUTERS AT THE MEETING

Since the personal computer is useful in organizing the meeting and assisting with follow-through assignments, why not bring the computer to the conference room? Many executives are doing just that, and the computer is turning in some dramatic results. During brainstorming sessions, you could have your personal computer booted with a spreadsheet program to add excitement and focus to the meeting. All those present around the table can perform "what if" analysis and know the results within seconds. You don't need to waste time performing manual calculations for every possible scenario.

Personal computers have their place at some meetings, but for other gatherings you would be well advised to leave your personal computer in your office. Personal computers are a great help during informal sessions that are held to generate ideas. They are less welcome, obviously, in high-level gatherings where participants receive advance notice of the kinds of information they are to bring. In this surrounding, bringing a computer may appear to some executives as if you have come to the meeting unprepared, especially when the presentation stops while the computer generates the necessary data. Handouts are still preferred for more structured meetings.

You may also see some frowns if you try to telecommunicate information from the company's mainframe computer to your personal computer during a highly structured meeting. Logging on and downloading the information can be disruptive, and any problems transmitting the data will be compounded as all the other executives stare while you try to retrieve the lost information. Bringing in information from a remote computer, however, can be impressive if the computer is stationed in a corner of the room and you or your assistant can step away to access the data without breaking the continuity of the meeting.

One of the best uses of a personal computer during a business meeting is to take the minutes of the meeting. An assistant can quickly input the transactions into a word processing program in the computer and shortly after the meeting print out copies for the participants. The major drawback with this application of a personal computer is that typing on a computer keyboard is more distracting than writing with pen and paper. Although the sound is certainly less disturbing than a passing jet, it could impede the discussion.

Should you bring your personal computer to your next meeting? Like other considerations of an effective meeting, bringing your computer will require careful planning well before the meeting date.

Is the meeting formal or informal? If it is formal, you will be well advised *not* to take your computer along. Even for an informal gathering you must be sure there is a convenient electrical outlet and a proper table to store the computer so it becomes a working tool of the meeting and not an annoying distraction. After all, your colleagues are not attending the meeting just to see how you operate a personal computer!

If you do decide to bring your personal computer to the

meeting, be sure that it won't let you down when it's your turn to be in the center ring. When you're ready to begin your presentation, your computer better be ready too. You do not want to turn in a disappointing performance because of delays caused by your computer.

Plan your moves well ahead of time. Rehearse your performance using your computer and, if possible, hold the rehearsal in the conference room where the meeting is to take place. Always conduct a rehearsal a day or two before the meeting. This will give you sufficient time to shape up your performance and fine-tune your interactions with your computer.

Your primary objective is to have a smooth interaction with the computer during your talk. For example, if you need to use the computer to make a point or retrieve data, do so while you are still addressing the audience. Preserve the continuity of your presentation while you are pressing the computer keys. It will take some practice before you master this technique, but it is worth developing. When you have perfected this technique, the participants probably will not notice that you are using a personal computer.

Perceptions

Business meetings are convened with the underlying purpose of persuading the participants to adopt a specific course of action. Whether you call the group together to hear a forecast of corporate growth or to kick off a multifaceted project, your job is to ensure that those present fully understand the important facts. With the proper information, those in attendance are encouraged to give their wholehearted support to the concept.

Here are a few factors professional communicators have found to assist presenters reach their audiences:

■ Audiences look more favorably on a presentation when they view the presenter as trustworthy and knowledgeable.

- Perceptions are more solidly based when audiences see the logic that has led up to the position presented at the meeting.
- If the presenter is really to convince an audience, he or she must be explicit in how the facts lead to the proposed conclusion.

Unless your audience strongly believes in the idea that is being proposed or can be convinced that the proposed policy is logically sound and will lead to the betterment of all, there is little chance that it will be carried out to the fullest extent. To gain the support of your staff or colleagues, you must carefully develop a strategy for each step of the adoption process. Here is a summary of the steps that are used to adopt an idea:

- A participant must become aware that the idea exists. The proposal must be presented in a creative way to help attract the participant's attention, making him or her feel that something new and exciting is happening.
- You must encourage the listener to seek more information independently. At this stage you must provide your colleagues with all the facts necessary to understand the proposal.
- Now the participant must review the material and decide whether or not to give the idea a try.

To be successful, you must monitor your audience during the entire meeting. Be sure that you have successfully guided your audience through each step of the adoption process before proceeding to the next phase of your presentation. Here are a few proven monitoring techniques:

- Encourage questions from the floor after you present a series of points.
- Watch the expressions on the faces of your audience. Be alert for participants who appear confused or seem to lose interest in your presentation.

- During a break in the meeting, informally question a few of the participants on the ideas that you presented.

- Any weak points that you detect in the adoption process must be reinforced with more facts to support the proposed concept.

The key to a successful presentation is your ability to communicate effectively with the audience. Convincing your colleagues to support the proposal on the floor requires both factually supported information and good communication skills.

Professional communicators are aware of how important the attitude and awareness of the listeners are to the effectiveness of the communication process. The following are a few unofficial guidelines that can be used to help assure effective communication:

- The information you are presenting must be absolutely transparent. It must have the clarity that will enable everyone in the audience to follow along with the presentation.

- Your presentation must have a clearly defined purpose. The audience needs to know that they will learn something by attending the conference.

- During the presentation your text and illustrations must not stray from, or contradict, the purpose of the meeting. Repeated disgressions during a presentation will confuse the participants.

- The communication vehicle must be appropriate for the participants and for the objective of the meeting. For example, a sales meeting where objectives are displayed and discussed is perfect for a large group meeting. In comparison, performance review sessions where the difficulties individual sales people are having are discussed lend themselves to a one-to-one conference where the participants can be assured of relative confidentiality.

■ The audience must be able to understand what is being presented. This may sound simple, but it involves the audience's level of education, technical skills, and their attitude at the time of the presentation. There is a time and place where a person is more likely to be attentive to a communication, and it is up to you to create that environment.

Many things can block effective communication. Unfortunately, many of them are out of your control and, to a lesser degree, out of the control of the participants. Here are a few key obstructions to effective communication:

■ Time limitations are a common problem in communicating. Is there sufficient time for you to communicate your ideas and for the participants to digest the information being presented?

■ Fear is another hindrance to audience support. This is especially evident when the topic of discussion can, if enacted, substantially alter the participant's normal routine.

■ Outside pressures on you and your audience. Your meeting and proposal are just two of the many items that must be handled within the workday. You must compete with these other influences to get the audience interested in the subject matter being presented. In some cases, the competition may be stiff.

Experienced communicators have learned that staff members are most attracted to topics that touch them personally. A discussion about personnel benefits will usually elicit intense interest from participants while a discussion about a technical change in a product with which they are only nominally involved will be of little interest.

It is the presenter's job to make sure that the topic of conversation is personalized to the audience. If the participant is only remotely involved with the subject, it is up to the presenter to show clearly how the participant will be affected. If you anticipate major problems, then you should reconsider holding the meeting, consider changing the topic of discussion, or consider not inviting those who don't have a personal need for the information.

When you announce your meeting, the staff members you invite may not be able to tell whether your meeting is important enough to justify interrupting their normal routines. Your initial memos may not contain enough specific information to persuade everyone to attend. At times busy executives decide to come simply because the person holding the meeting is a high-ranking officer in the company. If you don't have that kind of pull, it is up to you to convince your colleagues, long before the meeting convenes, that your presentation is important.

Presentations

Here are a few points, critical to all presentations, that can be used to assess your presentation material:

■ A good presentation must communicate a substantial, relevant message that is worthwhile to both the presenter and the audience. Discussions that dwell on insubstantial, trivial topics will lead to dissatisfaction among the participants, and they will quickly lose interest in the discussion. Today's executives simply don't have time to waste!

■ As the presenter, you must have a positive attitude toward your proposal. You must be completely sold on the idea you are presenting and convinced that there is no better solution available. Your audience must come away with the feeling that your proposal is the best approach. If you are not positive, your lack of confidence will be picked up by your colleagues, and this will certainly lessen the value of your presentation. If you don't believe in it, why should your audience?

■ Your presentation must accomplish two critical goals: It must be factually comprehensive and yet simple

enough so everyone leaves with a complete understanding of your proposal. The discussion must cover
all of the information necessary for your audience to
come away with a thorough understanding of the basic
facets of your proposal. Yet you must not overload your
presentation with complicated details; these can be
covered later in your follow-up memos.

The best place to start when planning your presentation
is with your audience. In most situations, you will know in
advance the types of people who will be attending the
meeting. For example, you will know their job titles and the
functions they perform within the corporation. This information alone is not sufficient to help prepare your discussion. You must have detailed knowledge of your audience:

- Are they familiar with the topic to be discussed?
- What level of knowledge does each member of the audience possess? Do some general managers have little
  technical knowledge and are others engineers?
- Must you provide introductory information to bring
  certain members of the audience up to a uniform level
  of knowledge?
- Do they know about your background? Will you have
  to include in your presentation some personal information that will convince them of your expertise?
- What do they expect to hear? Will any of your ideas
  be poorly received?
- What kind of an audience will they be? Are they already sold on the facts that you are going to present
  or will you be fiercely challenged from the floor?

Once you have answered these questions about your audience, you will be in a better position to prepare your presentation material. You can anticipate the questions that they
will ask and make sure you cover them in your talk.

When preparing the text for your presentation there are
a few guidelines you should follow:

- Develop your speech as if you were talking to one person. Although you will be speaking before many staff members, each member of the audience is seeing only one face—yours.

- Regardless of your position in the company, you must speak to the participants as equals. Don't talk down or up to them. This can only lead to poor communication.

- Use the most straightforward, simple words in your presentation. Avoid terms or phrases that may be vague or unfamiliar to some of the participants. Your objective is to communicate effectively, not to impress anyone with your vocabulary.

- You should include just enough facts in your speech to support your position. Overloading a discussion with extraneous facts only leads to confusion.

- You should avoid using complex math in your illustrations. They should be simple pictures that everyone, regardless of their background, will be able to understand with the help of your explanation.

Although you have carefully prepared your presentation, there are several points that must be considered about the delivery of the presentation:

- Use your normal tone of voice. If you are reading from a prepared text, be sure you speak using natural inflections in your voice.

- Maintain as much eye contact as you can with your audience. Don't fall into the habit of reading from the script without looking up.

- Breath naturally during the presentation. Although you might feel nervous, breathing normally will lessen the chance that your anxiety will affect your speech.

- Avoid the traditional signs of an ill-prepared speaker. Speak clearly and don't say "uh" and "um." This only clutters the fine words that you have prepared.

- Body language gives the audience a clue as to your attitude and feelings. When you are giving your presentation, stand up straight and keep your hands above your waist.
- Feel free to use gestures during your speech.
- Most of all, show your interest in what you are talking about. Your enthusiasm will naturally flow to your audience.

There are many reasons why participants lose interest in the speaker's presentation. Some of these failings can be recognized by the speaker during the presentation and quickly corrected. You must constantly be on the lookout for hints from the audience that will indicate where your presentation needs a quick shot in the arm. Here are a few potential problems:

- The presentation is too long.
- There are not enough breaks.
- The discussion is beyond the interest of the audience.
- The speaker is hiding behind the podium, reading his or her speech in a monotone.
- There are too many irrelevant facts slowing down the presentation.
- The topic under discussion is not seen as very productive.

The meeting you plan can be a success if you follow the guidelines presented here, which are commonly used by professionals in the communications business. With each piece of the plan in place, you will be able to persuade your audience to support your ideas.

1

Overview: Creating Presentation Microcomputer Graphics and Art

WITH YOUR speech written, it is time to turn to the illustrations you will use to clarify and highlight important points. Presentations slides have a dual function: They visually represent your ideas and they hold the attention of your audience. An audience wants a presentation to be interesting and move along at a fast pace. A slide doesn't have to tell the whole story; it only has to illustrate a single fact. Many slides that build during your presentation can communicate your proposal effectively.

Professional speakers have found that a speech incorporating many slides, each shown less than a minute, will hold an audience's attention longer than a presentation with a few slides, each shown longer. The variety of slides also gives the audience something new to look at every few seconds. If your slides are of professional quality, your audience will be just as interested in seeing the next slide as they are in hearing each point of your presentation.

Until the development of the personal computer and presentation graphics software packages, executives were forced to seek the help of professional artists to create their slides. Time was spent conveying the objective of the presentation to the artist. Then the artist's first draft of the slide had to be reviewed and modified. A second draft was often necessary before final approval of the art was given. This sequence could be repeated dozens of time, one for each slide. Of course, the outcome was dramatic, but those slides were expensive to produce. Depending on the number of revisions, the company might pay the artist more than $100 per slide. This meant that a 15-minute presentation could cost several thousand dollars.

Today, slides can be developed for a fraction of this cost by using the personal computer in your office. Your personal computer can be converted into a slide maker and even a slide show machine through the use of software packages that have a one-time cost of from $30 to $400. For this price you can make as many slides as you need and create and modify them at your leisure.

There are four general categories of presentation software:

- *General-purpose software* enables you to produce a variety of art including diagrams, engineering drawings, and special illustrations.

- *Business graphics software* enables you to manipulate data and produce a visual presentation of this information.

- *Analytical graphics software* accepts information from databases and spreadsheet software, performs statistical analyses, and produces graphs.

- *Slide show software* can be used to organize and display illustrations created with other software packages.

Each category of software has a particular use and a varying degree of difficulty for the user. For instance, most general-purpose software requires that the user be more creative in the overall design of the illustration. The user is confronted with a darkened screen with a tiny dot in the center. By pressing control keys, the user is able to move the dot around the screen. Additional keys are used to fix the dot in a particular location on the screen. By arranging these dots in a series, the user creates a design on the screen.

For the average business executive, designing a slide using a general software package is too time-consuming and often frustrating. For a more artistic individual, this type of software package opens a wide range of creative possibilities.

Business graphics software is designed for the executive who wants to produce quickly a visual representation of data. Many of the integrated software packages like Lotus 1-2-3 have the capability of transforming data stored in a spreadsheet into a graph. With most business graphics software you don't have to have any artistic talent. Most of these software packages are menu-driven (all the steps you need to follow and the commands you need to use are presented by the software in a series of on-screen lists) and can create an at-

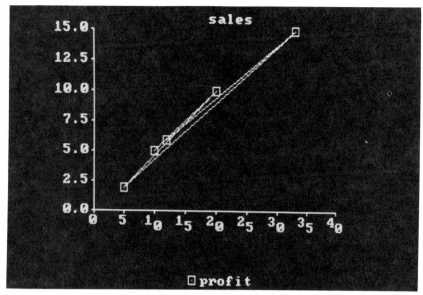

Business graphics software is capable of producing a variety of graphs, including pie charts, bar graphs, and the plotted curve illustrated here.

tractive slide in about 10 minutes. These programs are simple and fast to use.

Analytical graphics software combines two types of software—statistical and graphics. Software in this category will accept data from a spreadsheet program and offer the user the opportunity to perform a wide variety of sophisticated statistical calculations with the data. The result of this manipulation is then displayed in a graphic illustration.

Slide show software programs do not produce any charts or graphs. They don't analyze information. They are designed to accept illustrations that have been prepared using software from one of the other three categories and store them on a single disk. The user can then instruct the software to retrieve each illustration in a given order. The software package displays your illustrations in a smooth, flicker-free sequence. This category of software transforms your personal computer into a slide projector.

Three of the more popular business graphics software packages are Lotus 1-2-3, VisiTrend/Plot, and ExecuVision. They are available for many personal computers.

Lotus 1-2-3 is both a spreadsheet program and a graphics package. It can produce color graphics on your computer's display, and in up to seven colors using a plotter. Lotus 1-2-3 has some statistical capabilities, but these are limited to the more basic functions. Using Lotus 1-2-3 you can produce a bar graph, pie chart, stacked bar graph, and a plotted line. You can even overlay one graph on top of another. A useful feature of Lotus 1-2-3 is its ability to let you change and reenter data from the keyboard. When a series of data is changed, the software quickly redraws the graph. You can test your "what if" theories and see the results graphically displayed within seconds. In Chapter Four, we discuss in some detail how to use Symphony and Framework—more advanced versions of software like Lotus 1-2-3.

VisiTrend/Plot has many of the same features as Lotus 1-2-3 with a few notable differences. VisiTrend/Plot does not have a spreadsheet built into the program. Although you can enter data into this program from the keyboard, for all practical purposes you will require a spreadsheet program to use the data efficiently. VisiTrend/Plot also is limited by the type of hard-copy output it can produce. You can have VisiTrend/Plot copy the image on the screen to a printer, but not to a plotter.

ExecuVision, which we will discuss at length in Chapter Five, combines standard business graphics like pie, bar, and line graphs with state-of-the-art animation, color sketching, and high-quality clip art illustrations.

In the analytical category, a software package you might look into is *Graph N' Calc.* This is a serious software package that will permit you to enter data in the same fashion as you would using a spreadsheet software package. Graph

Presentation Graphics Software at a Glance

Graphics Software	Compatible with Computer(s)	Calculates Statistics	Creates Text Slides	Animation	Slide Show	3-D Rotation
EnerGraphics	IBM PC	YES	YES	YES	YES	YES
ExecuVision	IBM PC	YES	YES	YES	YES	NO
Executive Briefing System	APPLE II	NO	YES	NO	YES	NO
Frame Up	APPLE II	NO	YES	NO	YES	NO
Graph N' Calc	IBM PC	YES	YES	NO	YES	NO
HyperGraphics	IBM PC	NO	YES	YES	YES	NO
Screen Director	APPLE II	NO	YES	NO	YES	NO
Super Chartman II	IBM PC	NO	YES	NO	YES	NO
The Graphics Department	APPLE II	NO	YES	NO	YES	NO
Lotus 1–2–3	IBM PC	YES	YES	NO	NO	NO
Symphony	IBM PC	YES	YES	NO	NO	NO
Framework	IBM PC	YES	YES	NO	NO	NO
PC Draw	IBM PC	NO	YES	NO	NO	NO
PFS:Graph	APPLE II,III IBM PC	NO	YES	NO	NO	NO
VisiTrend/Plot	APPLE II,III IBM PC	YES	NO	NO	NO	NO

N' Calc, however, is not a spreadsheet program. Graph N' Calc has many of the forecasting calculations used by corporate business executives built in, such as internal rates of return and exponential smoothing. Graph N' Calc can also be used to create graphic representations of the data on your computer screen or output to a printer or plotter. If you don't want to enter the data into the Graph N' Calc spreadsheeting, you can use a file from a spreadsheet software package such as Lotus 1-2-3 or VisiCalc.

There are several good software packages available if you just want to produce a graphic illustration of the data generated by a spreadsheet program. One of these, *PFS:Graph,* enables you to use a variety of charts and line graphs to highlight your presentation. PFS:Graph can produce illustrations similar to the category of graphics software packages we discussed earlier. What makes PFS:Graph interesting is that you can mix the various styles of graphs and pie charts on the same screen. This is an ideal feature when you want to compare several sets of data on the same slide. Like the other packages, PFS:Graph will produce your illustration on the computer screen or on a dot matrix printer and a plotter.

Super Chartman II is another important chart-making software package. Like PFS:Graph, it will accept data created on a spreadsheet program and use this information to produce an illustration. But Super Chartman II has a unique feature. It can produce about 20 different styles of graphic illustrations as well as a few interesting three-dimensional charts that add a great deal to the presentation. It can reproduce these images on the screen or output it to a printer and to a plotter.

EnerGraphics, which will be discussed in more detail in Chapter Five, enables you to perform advanced statistical analysis to create all the standard business graphs and charts, and several state-of-the-art variations, such as three-dimensional bar charts with negative and multiple scales.

EnerGraphics can accept data from VisiCalc, Lotus 1-2-3, and Multiplan.

In the slide show category of graphic software packages there are a number of interesting products on the market.

The Executive Briefing System is a versatile product. This program really falls into several of the categories of graphic software. With it you can produce both text and graphic slides. You can choose from a wide variety of typeface styles and colors. And The Executive Briefing System has a function that lets you tie together all of the slides that you have developed into a slide show. On one disk you can store up to 32 slides. With The Executive Briefing System your personal computer can be transformed into a slide projector.

The Graphics Department is another good package. Like The Executive Briefing System, it falls into several categories. You can design slides using The Graphics Department by either entering data from the keyboard or from a data file produced by another software package. It has the software programs necessary to perform the basic statistical analysis that most business executives need, including regression analysis. Then it can change your personal computer into a slide-producing machine. The Graphics Department can produce more than 100 different colors and you can select from among 20 typeface styles. Finally, The Graphics Department can save the illustrations you create and allow you to call them up, creating a slide show.

If you have artistic talent, then you may want to design your own graphic art from scratch with one of the general-purpose graphics software packages. At the top of the list is The Graphic Solution. You can design whatever image you desire on the screen and save it on a disk. But don't expect too much help from the software; you must come up with the design yourself.

The Graphic Solution has a unique animation function, one of the more complicated features available that is sure to thrill your audience. With it you design a sequence of individual frames that creates the illusion of movement. For example, your first frame could show a traditional bar chart that compares your annual growth with that of your competition. Subsequent frames could dramatically illustrate your company's growth over a number of years to demonstrate the potential effects of your proposal. Your final presentation will inform and interest every member of your audience.

HyperGraphics is another highly sophisticated graphics software package and is more complicated than The Graphic Solution. Besides providing many of the features offered in The Graphic Solution, HyperGraphics will also allow another program to take control of it. For example, you can design your program and adapt the features of HyperGraphics without breaking into the HyperGraphics program. For most business executives, this capability exceeds their real needs. For others, however, it opens a whole new realm of possibilities.

Your corporation will find it economical to use the personal computer to create other forms of graphic art, such as flowcharts, engineering drawings, and floor plans. Although you can create any of these with a general-purpose graphic arts software package, there is one package that is designed to handle this function. It's called PC Draw.

PC Draw enables you to create special symbols such as those used in an office layout. Once these are stored on a disk, they can be recalled and used anywhere on the screen. Like other graphics software, PC Draw outputs the illustration to the screen and to a printer. Although most of the software packages we have discussed require the data to be entered either from a keyboard or from a data disk, PC Draw offers a third alternative, a light pen. This enables the user to draw symbols on the screen freehand. The computer then stores these images on a disk.

This is just a sample of the programs that are available in the personal-computer graphics field. In later chapters we will discuss in more detail how you can use these and other software packages to create reports, colorful graphs, and even a slide show.

The Monitor You Use Is Critical

Most computers are purchased with a monitor—usually a monochrome monitor. They cost several hundred dollars and provide displays of text and low-resolution graphics in one color. (Technically there are two colors produced by a monochrome monitor, the foreground and the background colors, but they are still referred to as single-color monitors.) These monitors are available in green, black and white, and amber. A monochrome monitor is ideal if you are working with word processing programs, spreadsheet software, and databases where color is not important.

However, if you are going to design presentation software, photograph images from the computer's screen, or use the computer as a slide machine, then you should purchase a color monitor. There are two types of color monitors available: composite video and an RGB monitor.

Both of these monitors will produce color images on the screen. However, the composite video monitor is best suited for general-purpose, low-resolution graphics. They are perfect for running most software, including business graphics where high resolution and exact colors are not critical. A composite color monitor is acceptable in a busi-

Although computer-generated graphics are more pronounced when displayed on a color monitor, the Panasonic TR-120MIP monochrome computer display will give you sharp images.

Although the type of color monitor you use will depend upon the computer you are using, displays like Panasonic's DT-S101 dual-mode color monitor accepts both composite and RGB video signals.

For the best color reproduction of business graphics, a high-resolution RGB monitor like the Panasonic DT-H103 is required.

ness setting when the final illustration will be produced using a dot matrix printer or a plotter. In this case the image on the screen is only used to assist in designing the slide and previewing the image before a hard copy is produced.

When you will be taking a picture of the image directly from the screen or showing the display to your audience, you will require very fine, high-resolution illustrations. For this you will need the more expensive RGB monitor. This type of monitor produces the sharpest possible image.

Your monitor, computer, and presentation graphic software are a team. When you select these members of the team, you must make sure that they are compatible with each other. There are monitors on the market that can display millions of different colors. You can purchase these and attach them to your personal computer, but you will still only be able to use the 4, 8, or 16 colors that your computer can generate. Take, for example, a typical IBM PC linked with an IBM color graphics adapter board (this is the circuit board that you need to add to your computer to produce a color image on the monitor). Regardless of the capability of your monitor, you can only produce 16 colors. That is the limit of the IBM color graphics adapter board.

Another important consideration is the resolution the monitor can accept. This is called the screen resolution and refers to the number of pixels that can be displayed on the screen. Typically, screen resolutions run from 300 × 260 to 1024 × 1024. The lowest resolution on a high-resolution monitor will produce close to 80,000 pixels on the screen. At the highest-level resolution there are over a million pixels. You should also check to determine the monitor's bandwidth. This is the rate at which the monitor can accept data from the computer, and it is measured in megahertz (MHz)—millions of cycles per second. Although the bandwidth for monitors ranges from 4.5 MHz to 50 MHz, you only need to match the MHz rating of the video output of your computer. For example, a monitor might be able to handle 50 MHz, but this excess capability is wasted if your personal computer can only send the data at 12 MHz.

When you are looking to purchase a monitor, the best thing to do is to visit your local personal-computer dealer and see the monitor in operation. If possible, have the dealer use the same presentation software during the demonstration that you will be using later in your office. Look carefully at the monitor, especially around the edges of the screen. The image should look sharp even along the edges. Then check the accuracy of the color guns inside the monitor. To do this, fill the screen with one letter and then set the screen to all white. Check each letter carefully to make sure that the entire letter is white and that the other colors are not fading into the letter.

Then turn all the adjustment knobs their full range and notice if there are any problems with each of these features. Sit down in front of the screen and work with both a presentation graphics software package and a word processing package. Are you comfortable working with this monitor? Do you notice even the slightest problem? If you do, keep trying monitors. Once you purchase the monitor, you will have to work with it for many months.

When you are looking for a monitor, you must keep in mind that you need to make an economical purchase. You don't have to buy the top of the line in graphics monitors unless you are preparing slides for a commercial television station. What's the right monitor? How much are you willing to spend? The best approach is to test the software and monitor at your local dealer. If the image on the screen suits your needs and the monitor has passed the quality checks we mentioned and, finally, if you have found the best price for the make and model of monitor that you want—buy it!

Color Monitors at a Glance

Monitor	*Type*	*Resolution*	*Bandwidth (MHz)*
Amdek Color I	COMPOSITE	260 × 300	4
Amdek Color II	RGB	560 × 240	12
Amdek Color IV	RGB	720 × 420	16
Hitachi HM1719B	RGB	720 × 540	25
Hitachi HM2713	RGB	720 × 540	25
Hitachi HM2719B	RGB	960 × 720	25
Hitachi HM3619A	RGB	1280 × 1024	45
Hitachi HM4619	RGB	1280 × 1024	75
NEC JC1203DHA	RGB	690 × 230	8
NEC JC1216DFA	RGB	620 × 240	10
NEC JC1410P2A	RGB	800 × 400	23
Sanyo DMC6500	BOTH	350 × 350	5
Sanyo DMC7500	RGB	480 × 288	7
TAXAN RGBvis III	RGB	630 × 280	18
Zenith ZVM131	BOTH	390 × 480	6
Zenith ZVM135	BOTH	640 × 480	20

Hands-on Experience

What is it like to use a presentation graphics software package? Is it as easy as the advertisements claim? Can they produce quality graphic output on the computer screen or on a printer or plotter? Everyone who has contemplated using a personal computer to generate presentation graphics should ask themselves these questions. Because of the relatively expensive price tags found on most of these packages and the "no return" policy, executive's should be very careful to investigate the capabilities of various software packages before making a purchase.

With some packages, generating business graphics is easy. They're designed specifically for that purpose. Inputting data and producing the graph is a simple task for the operator. Some simple software packages won't do anything more complex than generate bar graphs, pie charts, and other basic illustrations to depict business data. If you require elaborate illustrations, you will need a graphics package that will handle more than simple business graphics. This type of software is higher priced, more technical, and more difficult to operate. If you don't require complex presentation graphics software, then it will be more adventageous to use a package designed for simple business graphics. One such graphics package is *PFS:Graph,* a simple, straightforward program any executive can use.

- ☐ When PFS:Graph is first loaded into your personal computer, you will see a menu with six options from which you can choose. The first function is Define Chart. This function lets you specify the style of graph (i.e., bar graph, pie chart) you want the software to create.

- ☐ Once this is completed, you return to the menu and select the next option, Enter/Edit Data. When this selection is made PFS:Graph presents a table on the screen. Now you enter your data using the keyboard. After you finish entering the data, you press the control key and the letter *C*, and the software takes over from there. It returns to the main menu again.

☐ Press the selection Display Graph, and the software will pause for about 10 seconds before presenting the graph on the screen. The software automatically scales the data to assure that all of the information is represented in the illustration.

☐ To make changes to the data, you can return to the main menu by pressing a control character and selecting the Enter/Edit Data key. The table will appear again, displaying the data you previously entered. You can make any change you desire and then return to the main menu. Select Display Graph and the graph is modified according to the changes you made in the data table.

Even considering the amount of time this program takes to print a hard copy of the graph, PFS:Graph beats any corporate art department in turnaround time. A simple graph will take about 12 minutes to produce from the time the program is first loaded into the personal computer to the moment the printer produces a hard copy of the graph.

Less then a decade ago executives who wanted to utilize the advantages of computer graphics for their business presentations had to be computer programmers. These graphics programs were created using primitive commands the computer could understand. Confronted with unfriendly graphics software, executives removed themselves from direct contact with such software. They let computer professionals handle the job of getting graphics software to produce quality art. Some executives opted for the corporation's art department or an outside graphics studio to produce the presentation art by hand. Fortunately for the business community, software publishing companies noticed the difficulty that executives were having with computer graphics software and concentrated on designing software that produced professional results and were easy to use.

Before the software companies changed their approach, the only way you could use your personal computer to make graphic illustrations was to write your own graphics program in a programming language such as BASIC. BASIC is a friendly programming language that can be learned quickly by any computer novice. It is also available for most personal computers. For example, in BASIC there are commands like DRAW and COLOR that enable anyone to create graphic images on the screen. All the executive had to do was to compose the set of English words which the computer recognizes as instructions to perform specific tasks.

If you want to take the time to learn and experiment with your personal computer, you can still create charts and graphs and almost any other image on the screen by using BASIC. Some executives, in fact, enjoy being able to control every facet of their personal computers.

Most executives choose to pass up creating their own graphics program and will purchase one of the several presentation graphics software packages we have reviewed. Software makes it easy for the business executive to create graphic art on his or her personal computer. The output of these software packages is of sufficient quality for most presentations given by the executive.

What Can You Expect from Your Software?

The presentation graphics software package that you purchase should, at the very least, be capable of producing line graphs, bar charts, and pie charts. It should also be able to produce at least four trend lines on a single graph.

Another feature that you should look for in a software package is the ability to leave room for missing data points. For example, a typical application is comparing data and time for annual growth analysis. The vertical axis of the graph is scaled with the data. The horizontal axis is scaled with time, usually indicated by months or years. In some situations you may find yourself without enough data to fill in each month. For example, you have information for January, February, April, and May. Although the horizontal scale contains the names of the months from January through May, the graphics package should also automatically leave room on the chart for you to fill in the missing data later.

The software you purchase should be able to create and use files that are compatible with other graphics and spreadsheet software. The file format that has become the de facto standard for data files is called *DIF (data interchange file)*. This was first used in the spreadsheet program VisiCalc and later adapted by other spreadsheet and graphics software developers.

Obtaining approval from their superiors to purchase software packages often becomes a stumbling block for some executives. Chances are that if you don't use graphics in your present position, you will find it difficult to justify the expense of presentation graphics software to your manager. But if you do have a computer and do use graphics services now, you can probably make a good argument for enhancing your personal computer with this added feature. When combined with a good business graphics package, personal computers will produce results suitable for almost any application that an executive will have.

Here are a few points to use when selling the idea of purchasing the presentation graphics software package:

- The time you use to present your ideas to an artist is expensive and there is no guarantee that the results of those discussions will produce the illustrations you need.
- Additional revisions in the art can delay the project and increase the final price of the slide.
- Talking your ideas over with an artist may actually limit the alternatives available to produce the information in slide form. Usually the executive tells the artist what the slide should look like. There is little room for any creative discussion.

- The more artistic slides generally are expensive to produce manually.
- With a presentation graphics software package, the slide can be produced within a few minutes of the time the data are entered. Slides can thereby be produced on very short deadlines.
- Graphics packages usually offer a wide variety of illustrations that the executive can select for his or her slide.
- The need for changes in the slide can be recognized and modified almost immediately. There is no costly delay.
- The cost of a presentation graphics software package is usually less than the expense of producing a single slide presentation, and it is not a recurring cost.
- The presentation graphics software and the personal computer can be shared by many executives.

To help sell the idea for purchasing a business graphics package, you may want to enlist the help of your local personal computer dealer. You can have the dealer provide you with hard-copy samples of the output of some of the more popular business graphics software. You may also want to invite the dealer to your office with a copy of the program to give other executives firsthand experience with computer-generated business graphics. Seeing how easy and relatively inexpensive it is to generate illustrations on the personal computer in your office is enough to convince anyone to give approval of the purchase.

The Top of the Line

It is great that your computer can plot your data and insert them into a report, but when it comes to designing a sales form, an office layout, a new logo, or a flowchart, where are you? Back to pencil and paper or to the corporate art department.

Corporate executives who have been using the graphics capability of personal computers for a number of years have found that they pay for themselves:

- The time it takes for engineers and artists to draw illustrations can be greatly reduced by using a personal computer.
- Because of the ease with which illustrations can be combined with text in computer-generated reports, more technical illustrations are finding their way into documentation. Communication is improved.
- Engineering departments have found that there is a substantial cost saving using graphics programs for a personal computer over the large-scale system.

Prior to the purchase of several personal computers with graphics software, some corporations were paying up to $150 per page for technical diagrams. These were developed using a $400,000 computer system. With a personal computer and a plotter or dot matrix printer, the same results are being achieved for a fraction of the cost.

One common application of advanced graphics software for the personal computer is to help in designing floor layouts. A recent case illustrates how important this new tool can be. A company was moving into a new office building and the office manager wanted to give each employee his or her own cubicle. Because space is expensive, the accounting department wanted to squeeze as many people into each area as would reasonably fit. The planning and accounting departments could not agree about how much space was reasonable. The planning department wanted to give each person more space than the accounting department said was necessary.

To settle the disagreement, a manager in the planning department drew to scale a cubicle the size suggested by the accounting department. She drew all of the office furniture that would be required. There was practically no room for the employee to move around inside the cubicle. On seeing the illustration the accounting department agreed to increase the size of the cubicle.

Today there is new graphics software on the market that promises an end to pencil-and-paper drawings of every kind. Through the use of high-resolution color displays and 16-bit microprocessors, new computers can generate shapes, colors, and animation that not long ago were only available on computer systems costing upwards of $100,000. Now, with an initial investment of about $4000, you can have the necessary equipment to reproduce almost any design and allow your creative talents to experiment in all directions.

Computer graphics are seen frequently on television. The systems that generate them cost megabucks and involve months of training before the operator is comfortable enough to use the system. For industrial settings there are special computer systems called Computer Aided Design (CAD) that are used in the design of a variety of products, including the circuitry for personal computers. Until now, most of these systems cost well over $100,000.

A few years ago CAD software was made available to the personal-computer marketplace. Although the prices of these packages were well under the $100,000 mark of their "big brothers," the software still sold for several thousand dollars. Additionally, you were also required to pay another $750 for a graphics tablet to input the drawing into the computer. To this you had to add the cost of a plotter and, of course, the price of your personal computer.

In 1983 software designers recognized that there was a need to provide personal computers with more powerful graphics software. One of the first programs to give personal computers this capability was Apple Computer's *LisaDraw* for their Lisa personal computer. Instead of the expensive graphics tablet other software packages required, Apple uses a mouse. The user simply moves this little box (the mouse) around the table and the cursor moves around the computer screen. Best of all, this system only cost about $10,000 in 1983. Since that time the rapidly moving personal-computer market has changed radically. The price of the Lisa has dropped and is now sharing the spotlight with Apple Computer's Macintosh. The Macintosh has a comparable graphics program called *MacPaint* that sells for well under the price of the Lisa.

It is easy to understand the explosion in the field of computer graphics once you sit down in front of a personal computer and use one of these fascinating software packages. Once the program is in the computer, your imagination is the only limit to what you can create on the display screen. This is especially true if you use a mouse. With MacPaint you can draw a perfect circle on the screen with two clicks of the switch on the mouse. When MacPaint is loaded into the computer, a border appears on three sides of the screen. In the border to the left of the screen are various shapes that can be used in your illustration. In the border at the bottom of the screen are various shades, hash marks, and dots that can be employed anywhere on the screen. In the top border there are command positions which, when activated by the mouse, will enable you to return to the operating system of the computer, where you can load additional software.

The mouse and the cursor move simultaneously on the screen. In the borders, the cursor appears as an arrow. On the drawing area of the screen, it becomes a dot. This dot is like the point of a pencil. When the switch on the mouse is clicked once, the "pencil is placed on the paper." Whenever you move the cursor on the screen, it leaves a trail similar to pencil marks on paper. Another click of the mouse and the "pencil is removed from the paper," allowing you to move the cursor freely about the screen without leaving any trail.

Drawing a circle is easy with MacPaint:

☐ Move the cursor to the picture of the circle in the left border of the screen. With the cursor over the illustration, you press the switch on the mouse.

☐ Bring the cursor into the drawing on the screen, to the location where you want the center of the circle to be

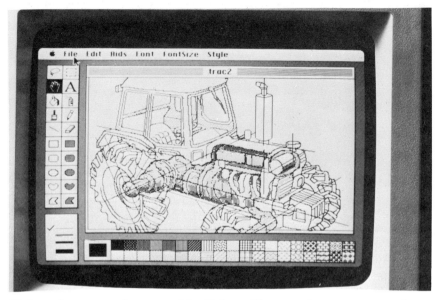

Using the many features MacPaint offers on its easy-to-use border menu, a talented operator can design impressive illustrations like this tractor.

    positioned. Press the switch on the mouse again to register the center of the circle in the computer.

☐ As you move the cursor away from the center, the computer automatically draws the circle, with the outer rim of the circle ending at the location of the cursor.

When you first use this feature, the image on the screen surprises you. You start off with a tiny dot, and with a simple move of the cursor a circle appears. Another click of the mouse and the circumference of the circle is fixed at the position of the cursor.

You can shade the inside of the circle just as easily. Move the cursor to the bottom border of the screen over the location of the shading that you want to use, pressing the mouse, and the computer will automatically produce that shade inside any shape that you select.

While Lisa's hardware/software combination was the first easy-to-use advanced graphics system to become widely

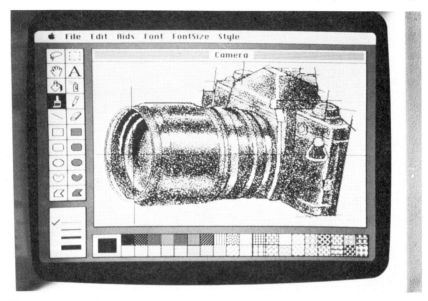

The shading feature available with MacPaint can be used to enhance your illustrations. This camera was given a realistic new dimension when the operator adroitly shaded areas of the image.

available, a host of new software packages for the IBM Personal Computer offer as much, if not more, functionality.

One advanced graphics software, *CADPLAN* from Personal CAD Systems in Los Gatos, California, is of particular interest to architects and industrial designers. CADPLAN is especially suited for professional, high-resolution illustrations. It has a 60,000 × 60,000-dot grid for its drawing area and offers 128 different pen sizes in three different colors. You can make drawings on 50 different levels, which is perfect for the architect who must separate such items as plumbing and electrical plans from the drawing.

Personal CAD Systems also has a powerful database linked to the graphics software. For example, suppose you want to build a wooden fence. You select a 1 foot × 8 foot piece of wood as your basic material for the fence. With this software you can draw a single piece of wood into position on the screen and have the software repeat the illustration for the length of the fence. Using the database, the software will tell you the number of pieces of wood that you will need for the project and the total cost for this material, once you tell it the cost of a single piece of wood.

CADPLAN also speeds up the drawing process by enabling artists to assign symbols to frequently used objects and store those symbols in the memory of the computer. While the artist is working on the drawing, he or she can quickly call up any of the symbols in the memory to be placed anywhere on the drawing. A less expensive version of CADPLAN has been produced by the same firm. It is called *CADRAFT*—this software offers only eight levels of drawings and does not have the database capabilities.

The range of business graphics that can be generated by your personal computer is extremely broad. Everything from simple bar graphs to the design of complex industrial products can be managed through the use of your personal computer. The combination of illustrations and text will make boring memos a thing of the past. Soon memos will include charts, diagrams, flowcharts, and perhaps even a drawing of a product. This new, enhanced form of office communication will not take you any more time or be any more expensive than old-style memos. They will be a great improvement over today's method of communication. Memos and other office communication will become more effective.

Advanced personal computer graphics software may take time to master and may be slightly more expensive than basic business graphics software, but the results are dramatic. They will capture the reader's attention and bring the message home.

2

Printers and Plotters —A Buying Guide

DEVELOPING AN attractive image on the screen of your personal computer is only half the task of producing presentation graphics. Unless you intend to photograph the screen you still have to capture that image on paper. There are several pieces of equipment that you can use: a dot matrix printer, a plotter, an ink jet printer, a thermal printer, or a laser printer.

Dot matrix printers draw your illustration by printing tiny dots on the page. Each dot represents a pixel on the computer monitor. With a plotter, pens are picked up by a moving arm and placed on the paper. Either the arm or the paper moves (depending on the type of plotter you use), tracing the image on the computer screen onto the paper.

Ink jet printers are similar to dot matrix printers except that, instead of impacting the paper as the dot matrix printer does, the ink jet printer shoots droplets of ink onto the page.

Thermal printers do not strike the page. Instead, they use heat-sensitive ink or paper to create the image. Heating elements are arranged in a matrix that coincides with the matrix position of the pixels on the screen.

Laser printers use office copier technology to reproduce your image. The laser receives signals from the computer and traces the image onto a drum inside the printer. This drum is similar to the drum used in office copier machines. Special ink, called toner, is transferred to the traced areas of the drum and rolled out on the paper. The toner is permanently fixed to the paper as the paper passes through a heating element.

Dot Matrix Printers—Great Value for Your Money

Buying a printer for your personal computer is probably one of the most important decisions you will make concerning your personal computer. You will be spending between $200 and $2000, depending on the type of printer needed for your application. Making such a sizable investment requires detailed planning and careful consideration before you visit your computer store.

There are several kinds of printers available for personal computers. We will take a look at dot matrix printers first, as they are the least expensive printers commonly used with personal computers. When you are shopping for a dot matrix printer, you should consider the following criteria before you make your purchase.

Paper Feed

Paper feed is the method used to feed the paper into the printer. Three types of paper feed are common: roll, tractor, and a combination of the two.

- A *roll feed* is identical to the method used to feed paper into a typewriter. The primary advantage of a roll feed is that you can use single sheets of paper (such as existing company forms) and you can change to different types of paper quickly. Roll-feed printers will require periodic adjustments to tighten the roller.

- *Tractor-feed* printers control the position of the paper via holes in the left and right margins of the paper that interlock with sprockets on the two tractor wheels attached to the printer. The advantage of this kind of paper feed is that you do not have to insert each sheet of paper, because the paper is on a continuous sheet. The primary disadvantage is that the printer will not accept single sheets of paper. All forms and letterhead stationery, for example, must be printed on continuous sheets of paper.

- Printers that feature a combination of the roll feed and tractor feed offer the best of both worlds without the major disadvantages.

Another important consideration when looking into dot maxtrix printers is the printer's ability to move the paper

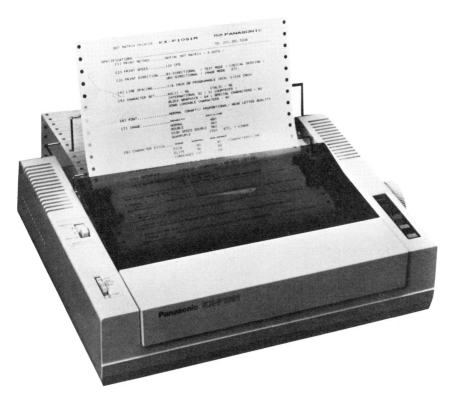

Panasonic's KX-P1091 is a typical dot matrix printer. It comes with both tractor and friction paper feed, and offers three printing modes (draft, near letter quality, and proportional spacing).

in both directions while the paper is in the printer. This allows you to align the paper easily with the printing head.

Ribbon Mechanism

The kind of ribbon mechanism used in the printer is also an important factor to consider. Dot matrix printers commonly use cartridge, spool, or loose ribbon.

■ The *cartridge ribbon* is cleaner for you to use. It is contained in a plastic case and slips easily into the printer without you having to touch the ribbon.

■ A *spool ribbon* requires you to thread the ribbon around the ribbon mechanism inside your printer. You'll find yourself washing your hands every time you replace one of these ribbons.

■ Few printers have the *loose-ribbon* arrangement. This system requires you to fan-fold the ribbon carefully onto a ribbon tray inside the printer. Similar to a spool ribbon, you'll have to thread the ribbon and clean yourself up after you're finished.

Printer Speed

Computers are fast and the printer you attach to your personal computer must be just as fast or your computer will be waiting for the printer to catch up. A printer's speed is rated by the number of characters that it prints in one second or the number of dots it can print when producing graphic art.

■ Slower printers only print in a single direction (left to right), with no printing taking place on the return of the printing head (right to left). Faster printers print in both directions.

■ Another critical factor to consider is the size of the printer's buffer memory. A printer can hold up to 10 pages of a document in its own memory, which allows you to use your personal computer at the same time the document is being printed. The larger the printer buffer is, the less time you will have to wait for the printer.

PRINTING IN STYLE

Dot matrix printers offer versatility in the style of the document that can be printed. Without changing the printing head, you can direct the printer through your word processing program and presentation graphics program to print in a variety of typefaces and type sizes. This gives you the capability to produce interesting printed copies.

Some dot matrix printers even allow you to design your own characters and symbols through the use of graphics software. This feature is called *dot addressable graphics* and is critical if you plan to use presentation graphics software with your printer. Dot addressable printers can also accept the standard character set from the computer. With the proper graphics software you can control the movement of every dot in the printing head.

Besides custom designs, some dot matrix printers can also produce characters and symbols used in foreign languages and notations used in math and science. If you need these special characters, be sure to check that the printer you intend to buy has this feature. Some printers are capable of producing only the standard character set found on the keyboard of the computer. Printers that are capable of accepting only standard character codes, called ASCII, are *not* suitable for graphics.

PRINTER AND SOFTWARE COMPATIBILITY

Although some printers have a wide variety of features to offer, these features can be utilized only if the proper commands are contained in the software program directing the printer. Unfortunately, there are some printer manufacturers who do not provide the necessary documentation with their printers to help you incorporate these features in the software you use. Similarly, some graphics software doesn't permit you to insert special printer command codes to take advantage of the unique features of the printer.

Before you decide on a printer, make sure there is sufficient documentation available, expecially on how to activate special features. Don't accept a demonstration of the printer by a dealer as a guarantee that it will work with your software. Some demonstrations consist of the printer producing standard character sets in various print styles without being attached to the computer. This is called an *automatic test* and is primarily used by service technicians to isolate trouble with the machine.

When you visit the dealer, bring along the software that you will be using and test it out with the printer. Let the dealer show you how to use the various print features. Seeing is still the best proof that the software, your computer, and the printer will work smoothly together.

SERVICE CALLS

When your computer system malfunctions, don't rush out to replace it. Usually just one component needs fixing, and it is up to you and a service technician to determine which component is at fault.

To help find the problem, some printers contain an on-board self-test. When the self-test is run, the printer will produce a printout of all the standard characters. You can use this self-test yourself before you call the technician to determine if the difficulty is with the printer. Usually, if the self-test produces all the characters, the problem is not within the printer.

It is not difficult to activate the self-test on a dot matrix printer. On many printers the test is started by depressing the function buttons on the front or top of the printer while the power switch is turned on. Other printers have a tiny switch inside the computer, called a dip switch. Turning this switch to the "on" position will place the printer in the test mode. If these techniques don't work with your printer, check the documentation that came with your printer for the proper procedure.

To reduce the chances of a breakdown, you should consider the type of mechanism used in the printer to move the printing head. There are three common mechanisms: belt drive, cable drive, and direct drive.

■ A *belt-drive* system is similar to the belts used in your automobile to drive the fan and air conditioner. Belts on printers occasionally must be adjusted to provide the proper tension for the printing head. You can perform these minor adjustments yourself. Other adjustments may have to be performed by a service technician.

- A *cable-drive* printing head is somewhat less likely to need adjustment, since this mechanism uses a cable that won't stretch.

- The best printing head drive, however, is the *direct drive.* The printing head mechanism is driven by a series of gears and normally no adjustments are necessary.

Beware! There can be hidden ongoing expenses when you use a dot matrix printer. There are normally two areas where expensive surprises can pop up if you are not careful: the price of ribbons and the cost of servicing the printer.

You might assume that the cost of ribbons for a printer is a minor matter. Unfortunately, this is not necessarily the case. Some manufacturers have used specialized ribbon mechanisms in their printers which require special ribbons. Chances are that you'll be paying a premium for this special requirement.

Ask your dealer how many characters can be printed using one ribbon. This information is one measure of the quality of the ribbon. With this information, and knowing your printing needs, you can estimate the number of ribbons you will need—and the price you will have to pay. Also check into the availability of the ribbons at your local dealer. It can be frustrating to learn after you use your last ribbon that is will take a couple of weeks before the dealer's replacement stock will arrive.

Another major expense can be the cost of servicing your printer. Some computer dealers who claim to repair the printers they sell, repair very little, if anything. Normally the dealer will package your printer and send it back to the manufacturer—something you can do yourself! The real surprise may come when you receive your repair bill. Some printer manufacturers have a flat fee for servicing a printer regardless of the problem. If the printer has a serious problem such as a blown circuit board, the flat rate may save you money. However, if your problem involves a minor adjustment, the bill could give you a shock.

Before you buy, check to see what service facilities are available. Be sure that your investigation includes a call directly to the customer relations department of the printer manufacturer to determine if it will be cheaper for you to send it to them directly.

THE FINAL LINK

Dot Matrix printers, like other computer peripherals, cannot be connected directly to your computer. Instead, you will require an interface card to make the final link. An interface card is a circuit board that is installed inside of your computer. Then you connect a cable between the interface card and the printer. The interface card actually handles the data communication between your computer and the printer. The most common printer interfaces are serial and parallel. When purchasing a printer, be sure that you ask the computer dealer which interface card you will require and whether the dealer sees any problems with using the printer you have chosen with your computer.

GRAPHICS AND DOT MATRIX PRINTERS

There are two standard techniques used to create graphic images using a dot matrix printer: bit mapping and vector information.

In *bit mapping,* the computer scans the screen for the position of each pixel under the direction of the graphics software package that is being used. This information is then stored in memory and sent to the printer. Bit mapping does have a major drawback—it uses a lot of the computer's memory to store the location of each pixel. This is compounded even more if you are producing high-resolution graphics, because a high-resolution illustration contains many pixels. After the video information is in memory, the program transfers this information, byte by byte, to the printer. This technique is referred to as a *screen dump.*

Although bit mapping is the most common method used for transferring images from a computer screen to a printer, there is another technique that will achieve the same results but requires less memory to function. This is called *vector information.* Instead of copying the position of each pixel, in vector information the software instructs the printer to draw a line of a specified length. The software gives the printer a starting and ending position for each of the lines. For all practical purposes, the results are the same as with bit-mapping technique.

Some dot matrix printers offer the capability of printing in color through the use of a multicolor ribbon. The ribbon contains four colors: cyan (a greenish blue), magenta (a deep purplish red), yellow, and black. Although the selection of these colors may seem odd, when they are arranged in the appropriate combination, they produce red, green, and blue. Dot matrix printers produce colors in one of two ways: Either the printer produces one color at a time with each pass of the print head (this is a slow process since the head must make several passes over the same line before the full color for the line is printed) or the printing head remains in one position until all the colors have been printed on that area of the paper. This is called *overstriking.* The printer will then have produced all of the colors on the line with just one pass of the print head.

QUALITY IS NUMBER ONE

The quality of a printed graphic page is rated in the same way as the resolution of an image on the screen—dots per inch. A printer that can produce a higher number of dots per inch (also called density) will produce a better-looking image. The quality of a dot matrix printer is also rated according to the number of dots per inch in an 8-inch-wide section of line. For example, a printer that can produce 72 dots per horizontal inch will have a 576 dot-per-line rating. A resolution of 72 dots per inch (both vertically and horizontally) will produce good illustrations. A printer with double this density will turn in an outstanding performance, while a printer with half that density will produce grainy, low-quality illustrations.

When you are investigating dot matrix printers, you must keep in mind the resolution of both your monitor and your personal computer. They must be within the same resolution tolerance. For example, a monitor that can produce 320 horizontal pixels on the screen will not be able to take advantage of the 576 dot-per-line capability of the printer. In fact, you may not be at all pleased with the resulting printed image. The full image on the screen will take up only 5 of the 8 inches on the page produced by the printer because of the difference in the resolution of the two pieces of equipment. The software and the computer copy the positions of the pixels onto the printed page.

Ink Jet Printers

Ink jet printers are the most widely used nonimpact printers available for personal computers. As the name implies, images on the paper are created without the printer striking the page. Except for the printing head, the ink jet printer operates almost the same as the dot matrix printer. Instead of tiny rods, an ink jet printer has between 4 and 12 tiny nozzles that spray droplets of ink onto the paper under the direction of the graphics software and the personal computer. Each nozzle is connected to a central inkwell from which it draws the ink. Each drop of ink that appears on the page represents a pixel on the computer screen. This process is identical to that used by a dot matrix printer to produce an image on the page.

Ink jet printers will not work properly with all types of paper. You should not use glossy paper or transparencies with an ink jet printer, as they are not absorbent enough

Ink jet printers, like Canon's PJ-1080A, shoot droplets of ink from fine nozzles situated in the print head.

and the ink will not properly adhere to the paper. This is a limiting factor. However, manufacturers of ink jet printers are expected to overcome this problem in the near future. For best results, manufacturers recommend that a high-grade bond paper with a very smooth natural surface be used with an ink jet printer. A rough surface will cause the ink to spread unevenly on the paper, reducing the clarity and the power of the graphics.

Another problem with ink jet printers is that the ink can dry out, especially when the printer is not used frequently. The reservoir is not the only place where the dried ink can cause problems. Ink can also dry out in the tubes leading to the nozzles and in the nozzles themselves. Although cleaning will usually return the printer to operating condition, some printers may require a new reservoir, tubes, and nozzles.

Ink jet printers can produce color. Similar to a dot matrix printer, four colors are used: cyan, magenta, yellow, and black. From these a variety of other colors can be created, although the color will not be as vivid as color graphics done on a dot matrix printer. There are four reservoirs in a color ink jet printer, one for each of the colors. The process used to place the color image on the paper is identical to that of a dot matrix printer; either the printing head prints one line of each color with each pass of the head or more than one color is printed in an area before the printer moves on to the next area.

Ink jet printers are not known for their speed; in fact, they are slow when compared to a dot matrix printer. A typical ink jet printer with four nozzles, for example, will print about 70 dots per inch and about 37 characters per second. An ink jet printer with 12 nozzles will print 120 dots per inch and 240 characters per second. The quality of an ink jet printer is also determined by the number of dots per inch. An ink jet printer producing about 70 dots per inch can be considered medium resolution, while a high-resolution printer produces 120 dots per inch. As with a dot matrix printer, the number of dots per line on your ink jet printer must be matched to the number of horizontal pixels that appear on your monitor.

Thermal Printers

Thermal printers use tiny rods to produce a pattern of dots on the paper, but unlike a dot matrix printer, the rods don't strike the paper. Instead, the rods are heated, which causes the portion of the chemically coated paper near the rod to turn black.

Thermal printers are inexpensive. However, they are not very well suited for office use. This is primarily because of the paper the printer uses. You cannot print on your existing forms, and the chemically treated paper is certainly not desirable for business correspondence.

Although the present thermal printing technology is of limited use to the business community, a different method is being examined by some printer manufacturers. With the new method, called *thermal-transfer printing*, the printing head pins heat up and melt the ink on a ribbon, causing a dot of ink to appear on the paper.

Thermal-transfer printers allow you to use any kind of

paper with the printer, since the ink is contained in the ribbon. Thermal-transfer printers are also much faster than regular thermal printers. Because of the time it takes for the chemical reaction to occur, a typical thermal printer is only capable of producing 30 characters per second. In comparison, a thermal-transfer printer can produce up to 500 characters per second.

Thermal-transfer printers do have a major drawback—their price, which ranges from $2000 to $4000. The ribbons are also expensive, costing approximately $30 apiece. This could cool rapid adoption of this type of printer in the industry, especially since there are less expensive alternatives on the market.

Another nonimpact printer that has drawn some interest from business executives is the electrosensitive printer. The printing head of this printer contains tiny needles made from tungsten. As each needle is designated by the software and computer to be activated, it discharges a small amount of electricity. Paper that has been coated with a thin sheet of aluminum is struck by the electricity from the needle and the aluminum is burned away, exposing the ink.

Electrosensitive printers have one major drawback: They can only print on special paper. But this is a mixed blessing. Because the paper is backed with aluminum, it is not easily destroyed, which makes the paper ideal for records that must be kept for long periods of time. Furthermore, it is not easy to counterfeit documents that are produced on electrosensitive paper. Items like theater tickets can be produced using this paper, making it nearly impossible for anyone to duplicate the ticket.

Laser Printing

Although certain parts of the technology have been around for many years, the art of laser printing is relatively new. The laser contained inside the printer receives impulses from the software and the personal computer; these impulses are actually on/off signals. When the computer sends the laser a signal to print a dot, the laser is turned on for a fraction of a second. The beam of light from the laser strikes material on a photosensitive drum. The drum rotates near a reservoir of black powder called toner, the same toner that is used in office copying machines. The toner is attracted to the areas of the drum that were struck by the laser. As the drum continues to turn, it deposits the toner onto a piece of plain paper. Toner is heat sensitive, so that when the paper carrying the toner passes through a heat source in the printer, the toner adheres to the paper. In addition to paper, a laser printer can also transfer images onto transparencies.

Laser printers can also print in color. The process used to produce a color image is very similar to the one used in offset printing. Toner of different colors is used, and with each pass of the drum a new color is added to the paper.

There are some real advantages to using a laser printer, such as working quietly without disturbing others in the work place. Most important, you can service most laser printers yourself. The entire imaging system is contained in an enclosed unit that can be slipped in and out of the printer smoothly.

Before you can use a laser printer to produce graphic art, however, you will have to purchase an image processor controller for your printer. Check with your local computer dealer to determine whether the laser printer you have in mind is designed to handle presentation graphics.

SELECTING THE PRINTER FOR YOU

All the printers that we have mentioned will enable you to reproduce images that appear on your computer screen. Some, such as the dot matrix printer, can do this quickly and economically. Others printers, such as thermal-transfer printers and laser printers, are still new and expensive.

Whenever you look for a printer you must examine its ability to produce high-resolution graphics. These printers may cost close to $1000, but they will pay for themselves, especially if you frequently have presentation graphics prepared by an independent artist.

Once you have decided on a particular printer, hold off from making the purchase until you have looked into two additional areas of importance: the warranty and the price. The warranty offered by the manufacturer should be considered with care. Although at first the warranty may appear to be written in language only an attorney could understand, it does describe how well the manufacturer will stand behind the product. Many printer manufacturers offer a 90-day warranty on parts and labor. But be careful! Some warranties may only cover parts but not labor. Read the warranty with care before you write the check for the printer.

The amount of money you pay for your printer will depend on where you make your purchase and how well you shop around. Buying a printer is like buying a television: Once you decide on the brand and model, you have to look for the best price. Although many computer dealers will quote you the list price of the printer when you first inquire, you can probably do better. Be sure you bargain; you'll be surprised by the price you and the dealer will settle on.

A local computer store may not be the best place to get the best price. You should keep abreast of advertisements from mail order companies. At times, dealing with a mail order firm can save you a few dollars on the identical printer you saw at your computer store. Before you buy your printer through a mail order company you should make a thorough price comparison. There are hidden costs when you buy through the mail. The price of the printer listed in the ad may be altered by the addition of such costs as shipping and handling charges. You should include these factors as you estimate the cost of the printer.

Selecting the right printer for your application takes planning, a basic knowledge of printers, and, finally, a test with your presentation software, a similar personal computer, and the printer of your choice.

The Plot Thickens

Most printers that work with personal computers produce graphic illustrations using patterns of dots to create the image. These graphics are suitable for many business situations. However, there are times when you want high-quality illustrations for a presentation. Graphic art that looks as if an artist drew it can give your presentation a polished, professional appearance. For this kind of quality you will need a *plotter* that actually draws your illustration. A plotter can generate all the standard charts and graphs plus more elaborate illustrations including line drawings, flowcharts, and other complex patterns. All plotters can produce these images on either plain paper or transparencies.

Plotters offer the executive the greatest flexibility and high resolution. For example, most plotters give you a choice of pens. The clarity of the line drawn by the plotter is deter-

Panasonic's high-speed color printer, model VP-6802P, can translate a business graph on your computer screen into a colorful hard copy.

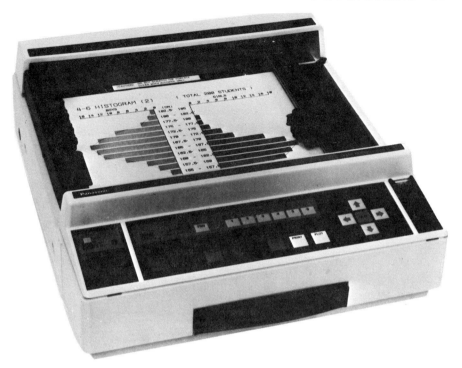

When you are giving presentations on the road, Panasonic's VP-6801 high-speed color plotter is an ideal traveling companion.

mined by the type of pen used. For less critical work, felt-tip pens can be installed in the arm of the plotter. Felt-tip pens will produce acceptable results that look as if you used a felt-tip pen with a template. The only disadvantage of felt-tip pens is that the lines on the page can be fuzzy around the edges. However, this is noticeable only if you take a close look.

Felt-tip pens produce the least professional-looking line. Hard-tip pens, such as a ball-point pen, will enable the plotter to draw more clearly and distinctly. Best results are achieved by using a pen that has a machined tip. The tip, a fine tube, is designed to produce a perfect line of a specific width every time. The width of the line is referred to as its *weight* and is designated by a point scale beginning at zero, which is the finest line that such a pen can draw.

Regardless of the type of pen you use in a plotter, more than one pen is necessary to produce presentation art. Different pens are required for each color and each line width in your illustration. Some plotters are capable of working only with one pen at a time. To produce an illustration that requires several colors, for example, you have to change pens each time a new color is required. When you use a single-pen plotter, you have to monitor constantly the plotter's operation. Other plotters, however, permit the operator to store several pens on the plotter. When a color change is called for by the graphics program, the plotter automatically selects the proper pen and continues to draw the image, and you don't have to stand by while the image is being drawn.

HOW PLOTTERS WORK

There are basically three methods used by plotters to produce an illustration on paper or transparency. In some machines the paper is held in a stationary flat-bed tray while the pen, held in a bar above the paper, moves to generate the illustration. The second method is very similar, except that the pen held in the arm remains stationary while the tray moves the paper to draw the image. Both methods are common in plotters designed for use with a personal computer. Some more expensive plotters use a more sophisticated method. Here the paper is attached to a drum, and the drum and the pen move to draw the illustration.

When you are looking to purchase a plotter, there are a few items that should be checked to determine its quality. An important consideration is the number of addressable steps that are available per inch—how many points can the plotter put on the page per inch? The greater the number of addressable steps, the higher the resolution and the more versatile the plotter. To produce acceptable business graphics, the plotter should have an addressable step rating of between 500 and 1000 steps per inch.

You should also check a plotter's ability to repeat itself

precisely. The plotter must be able to return the pen to the same position where it was just working. This function is critical in producing quality graphic art. For example, a good plotter can return the arm to the exact position when a change of pen takes place. The repeatability rating of a plotter is given with two sets of criteria: if the same pen is being used and if the pen has been changed. In either situation, the rating is given as a decimal number; the lower the number, the higher the quality of the plotter will be. A rating of 0.001, for example, is a good repeatability rating for a plotter.

Speed is another important factor to consider when you purchase a plotter. Unlike a printer, a plotter's speed is determined by the number of inches per second it can draw. An acceptable range is between 4 and 15 inches per second. Plotters are not necessarily fast, especially some low-priced plotters designed for personal computers. For example, a chart that contains both text and numbers coupled with a great deal of solid area can take more than half hour to produce. A more expensive, faster plotter can produce the same type of illustration in less than 15 minutes.

A PLOTTER OR A PRINTER?

Which is better for your situation, a plotter or a printer? If your work requires that you produce high-quality presentation graphics on paper or transparencies, you should purchase a high-speed plotter that uses machined pens that will give you the best results. A plotter with this capability is expensive and could cost more than $1500. However, for this one-time price you will have the capacity to produce high-quality graphics within 15 minutes. It is like having your own personal graphic artist on call around the clock.

If you don't need high-quality graphics and can use good representative art for your presentation, then you should look for either a lower-priced plotter or a dot matrix printer. If color is critical to your presentation, then purchase a multicolor, low-cost plotter. In some business situations, you may want to incorporate a chart or graph on the same page as text. The best equipment to use is a dot matrix printer. Here both text and graphics can be produced on the same page without slowing down the printing process.

IS A PLOTTER CHEAPER THAN AN ARTIST?

There are no hard statistics available to prove that a computer can beat an artist in generating business graphics. To determine which is really cheaper, you will have to perform a simple calculation:

- First, determine the amount of money you are considering investing in a computer, presentation software, and a printer or a plotter. (You might choose to amortize the equipment expense over its lifetime—usually five to ten years. However, the amortized cost does not reflect the actual cash outlay in the first year of operation.)

- Be sure to include maintenance items such as ribbons, film, pens, paper, and the price of a service contract.

- Include an estimate of the cost in wages for your staff to learn to use the software and printer or plotter. To do this, multiply the number of hours spent learning by the hourly wage of the operator and add this amount to the above costs.

- Divide the final dollar figure by an estimate of the number of business graphs you normally need each year. This total represents the fixed cost per slide.

- Then, multiply the average amount of time spent producing one graph (a simple graph takes approximately one hour to produce) by the hourly wage of the operator. This total represents the variable cost per slide.

- Finally, add the fixed cost per slide to the variable cost per slide to get an estimate of how much each graph will cost to produce in the first year of operation.

■ Now determine the current expense of producing business graphics using the services of a professional artist. This should also be estimated on an average cost-per-graph basis. Compare both expense estimates.

Although it is important to evaluate the cost of producing computer-generated art in-house (versus having art produced out of house), there are other considerations to ponder. For example, the expense of setting up an in-house operation will assure you of the use of only one system; if your personal computer, printer, or plotter malfunctions, your graphics production will shut down. In contrast, you can always reassign the project to a different artist, should one artist be unable to complete your job.

Another nonfinancial consideration in favor of using an artist is the wealth of creative ideas he or she can give you—usually at no additional expense. But an in-house operation is limited by the creativity of the operator and by the versatility of the presentation graphics software you use.

In the end, however, more and more executives are opting for computer-generated graphics because of the control and speed of production that computers make possible.

Graphic Printers

Company/Product	Type	Number of Colors
Advanced Color Technology —Chromajet Act II	Ink Jet	125
Alphacom		
—42	Thermal	none
—81	Thermal	none
Anacom General		
—150 (80 col)	Dot Matrix	none
—150 (132 col)	Dot Matrix	none
—150Z (80 col)	Dot Matrix	none
—150Z (132 col)	Dot Matrix	none
—160 (80 col)	Dot Matrix	none

Graphic Printers (*continued*)

Company/Product	Type	Number of Colors
—160 (132 col)	Dot Matrix	none
—160Z (80 col)	Dot Matrix	none
—160Z (132 col)	Dot Matrix	none
Anadex		
—DP 9000A	Dot Matrix	none
—DP 9001A	Dot Matrix	none
—DP 9500A	Dot Matrix	none
—DP 9501A	Dot Matrix	none
—DP 9620A	Dot Matrix	none
—DP 9625A	Dot Matrix	none
—DP 9725A	Dot Matrix	4
—WP 6000	Dot Matrix	none
—DP 6500	Dot Matrix	none
Apple		
—Imagewriter	Dot Matrix	none
—Silentype	Thermal	none
Atari		
—1025	Dot Matrix	none
—1020	Dot Matrix	4
BMC USA		
—PB 101	Dot Matrix	none
—PB 401	Dot Matrix	none
—BX 80	Dot Matrix	none
Canon USA		
—PW 1080A	Dot Matrix	none
—PW 1156A	Dot Matrix	none
—PJ 1080A	Ink Jet	7
Centronics Data Computer		
—Print Station 358	Dot Matrix	7
—122 Graphics	Dot Matrix	none
CE Terminals		
—CL 300	Dot Matrix	none
—CL 600	Dot Matrix	none

Company/Product	Type	Number of Colors
C Itoh		
—Prowriter 8510	Dot Matrix	none
—Prowriter 1550	Dot Matrix	none
—Prowriter 8510 S	Dot Matrix	none
—Prowriter 1550 S	Dot Matrix	none
—Prowriter 8510 SC	Dot Matrix	7
—Prowriter 1550 SC	Dot Matrix	7
Data Impact Products		
—DIP 84G	Dot Matrix	none
—DIP 92	Dot Matrix	none
Dataproducts		
—Pinnacle 8010	Dot Matrix	none
—Pinnacle 8060	Dot Matrix	7
—P 80	Dot Matrix	7
—P 132	Dot Matrix	7
Datasouth		
—DS 108	Dot Matrix	none
—DS 220	Dot Matrix	none
Diablo		
—Series C	Ink Jet	7
Docutel/Olivetti Information Services		
—PR 2300	Ink Jet	none
Envision		
—420	Dot Matrix	4
—Vector 430	Dot Matrix	4
Epson America		
—MX 80FT	Dot Matrix	none
—MX 100	Dot Matrix	none
—RX 80	Dot Matrix	none
—FX 80	Dot Matrix	none
—FX 100	Dot Matrix	none
Facit Data Products		
—4510	Dot Matrix	none
—4512	Dot Matrix	none

Graphic Printers (*continued*)

Company/Product	Type	Number of Colors
—5000 C	Dot Matrix	none
—5000 V	Dot Matrix	none
—4542	Dot Matrix	2
—4544	Dot Matrix	8
—4570	Dot Matrix	none
Genicom		
—3014	Dot Matrix	none
—3024	Dot Matrix	none
IBM		
—Graphics	Dot Matrix	none
—Compact Printer	Dot Matrix	none
Infoscribe		
—1000	Dot Matrix	none
—1200	Dot Matrix	4
Integral Data Systems		
—Prism 80	Dot Matrix	8
—Prism 132	Dot Matrix	8
—Micro Prism	Dot Matrix	none
Lear Siegler		
—Versa Print 500	Dot Matrix	none
Mannesmann Tally		
—MT 160	Dot Matrix	none
Micro Peripherals		
—Printmate 150	Dot Matrix	none
—99	Dot Matrix	none
NEC Home Electronics		
—8023 A	Dot Matrix	none
—Thermal Printer	Thermal	none
NEC Information North		
—7020	Dot Matrix	none
—7030	Dot Matrix	none
—7040	Dot Matrix	none
—7065	Dot Matrix	none

Company/Product	Type	Number of Colors
Okidata		
—Microline	Dot Matrix	none
Ope Printers		
—JP 101	Ink Jet	none
Panasonic		
—KXP 1090	Dot Matrix	none
—KXP 1160	Dot Matrix	none
Printacolor		
—PG 1000	Dot Matrix	125
Printek		
—910	Dot Matrix	none
—920	Dot Matrix	none
—930	Dot Matrix	none
Printronix		
—MVP 1508	Dot Matrix	none
Quadram		
—Quadjet	Ink Jet	7
Quantex		
—7030	Dot Matrix	none
—7040	Dot Matrix	none
Radio Shack		
—DMP 100	Dot Matrix	none
—DMP 200	Dot Matrix	none
—DMP 420	Dot Matrix	none
—DMP 500	Dot Matrix	none
—DMP 120	Dot Matrix	none
Siemens Communications		
—PT 88	Ink Jet	none
—PT 89	Ink Jet	none
—2712	Ink Jet	none
Star Micronics		
—Gemini 10X	Dot Matrix	none
—Gemini 15X	Dot Matrix	none
—SPX 80	Thermal	none

Graphic Printers (*continued*)

Company/Product	Type	Number of Colors
Texas Instruments		
—850	Dot Matrix	none
—855	Dot Matrix	none
Toshiba America		
—1350	Dot Matrix	none
Transtar		
—315/FC	Dot Matrix	7
Trendcom/3M		
—1902	Dot Matrix	none
—1912	Dot Matrix	none
—1904	Dot Matrix	none
—1914	Dot Matrix	none
Trilog		
—150	Dot Matrix	none
—300	Dot Matrix	none
—301	Dot Matrix	none
—302	Dot Matrix	256

Plotters

Company/Product	Pen Type	Color
Alpha Merics		
—Plot 1	felt	1
—Plot 2	machined	1
—Datascribe IV	machined	1
Amdek		
—DXY 100	felt	1
Apple		
—Color Plotter	felt	8
Bausch & Lomb		
—CPS	all types	4
—High Plot	all types	4

Company/Product	Pen Type	Color
BMC USA		
—XY Plotter	felt	4
Cal Comp		
—M84	ball point/felt	8
Comrex International		
—Comscriber	felt	12
Enter Computer		
—100	felt	1
—Six Shooter	felt	6
Hewlett Packard		
—7470	felt	12
Houston Instruments		
—Hiplot DMP 29	all types	8
Mannesmann Tally		
—PIXY 3	felt	8
Panasonic		
—VP 6801 A	ball point/felt	6
Radio Shack		
—CGP 115	ball point/felt	4
—CGP 220	felt	7
—FP 215	felt	4
Soltec		
—6801	all types	6
—6802	all types	8
—RY 10M	all types	8
—RY 1M	all types	6
Strobe		
—M 100	all types	1
—M 200	all types	1
—M 260	all types	8
Yokogawa		
—PL 1000	plastic	4
—PL 2000	fiber	4
—Graphmate II	fiber	4

3

Photographing Illustrations from the Monitor

AFTER YOU have manipulated the facts and figures you want to incorporate in your presentation and have developed an illustration on your computer, you still must generate a slide. You might use a printer or a plotter and take the printed illustration to a photographer who will make a slide for you. However, a slide of the printed copy will rarely match the image on your computer screen. Although the printed copy is a good representation of the screen, printers and plotters generally cannot capture the vivid colors or match the clarity of a high-resolution monitor.

The obvious solution is the use a 35-mm camera containing slide film to take a picture of the screen. If you have ever attempted to photograph an image on the screen of your television, you realize that the results are not always successful. One of the major problems with photographing the display of a personal computer occurs because of the way the monitor creates the image on the screen. When we look at the monitor, the illustration appears to be stationary, like a photograph. However, the image is not still at all.

Your monitor produces an image with a cathode-ray tube (CRT), similar to a standard television picture tube. The CRT consists of an electron gun and a glass screen coated with a chemical called phosphor. To create an image, the electron gun scans the screen from the upper left corner to the lower right corner, 30 to 60 times per second. During the scan, if the gun receives a pulse from the computer, it excites electrons that strike the screen, causing the phosphor to illuminate. The CRT creates images with tiny specks of illuminated phosphor in much the same way as a dot matrix printer uses tiny dots.

The image on the screen appears stationary because of the coordination of the scan speed and the decay factor of the phosphor. When a tiny dot on the screen is illuminated, the phosphor brightens and then eventually loses its illumination. For the image to remain constantly bright on the screen, the electron gun must fire an electron, scan the rest of the screen, and return to the same position to fire once more before the illuminated area dims.

Our eyes are not fast enough to catch the scan of the CRT. The scan occurs so quickly that the images overlay each other in our minds, creating the impression that we are looking at a single, fixed picture. A camera, however, cannot be misled this way. When the shutter of a camera opens to expose the film, anything in front of the lens will be captured. The shutter speed is critical to the quality of the image that will be reproduced on film. For example, when you photograph a youngster at play, you want the shutter to remain open for a short time to stop the action. If the shutter remains open for a longer period of time, the picture will be blurred. When you photograph an image on the monitor, you want to hold the shutter open long enough so the electron gun can complete an entire scan of the screen. The entire image on the monitor will then be captured on film. There are other aspects of photographing the screen such as lighting, glare, and the curvature of the screen itself. We will discuss these in more detail later in this chapter.

Photographing the Screen Using a 35-mm Camera

Photographing the screen using standard camera equipment is not as easy as pointing your camera at the screen and pressing a button. There is a difference between shooting a roll of slide film at a family gathering and capturing the image from a computer screen. Your first step is to make sure that you have all the necessary equipment. You will need a 35-mm single-lens reflex camera that you can adjust manually. You will need to look through the lens of the camera while framing the subject. The manual mode is necessary to enable you to adjust for glare and light. The camera lens will be open for almost a full second, so you need a tripod and cable release. Any movement will cause images on the slide to blur.

The lens you use on the camera is a critical factor in photographing the screen. Some 35-mm cameras are sold with a good, general-purpose 55-mm lens. This lens is usually *unsuitable* for photographing computer-generated art, because you cannot get a crisp close-up image of the screen.

There are several alternatives to the standard 55-mm lens. You can purchase a close-up lens attachment that will increase the focusing ability of the standard 55-mm lens. The only disadvantage is that you have to place the camera so close to the computer monitor that you won't have room to manipulate the computer. Or you may want to use a macro lens. This lens allows you to take full-screen shots with very little distortion. You can purchase a macro lens by itself or purchase a multifunction lens that has a macro feature. Many zoom lenses have this macro capability.

Once you have gathered all of the equipment, you line up camera and tripod directly in front of the monitor. Use the viewfinder to make sure that the camera will only pick up the image on the screen and not the monitor itself. You might want to find a horizontal line in the illustration and line this up with the top or bottom of the viewfinder. Adjust the position of the camera or the position of the monitor until they are properly aligned.

You can use any kind of slide film that is available for your camera. The type of film you use will have an effect on the color that will appear on the slide. For example, you can make the image more blue if you use Ektachrome 160 Tungsten. Some illustrations take on a more pleasant appearance if given an overall bluish effect.

Another critical factor in filming the image on the monitor is the exposure; too much or too little can detract from the illustration. The best way to determine the proper exposure is by experimenting.

Write down all the possible exposure settings that are available on your camera. Adjust the brightness and contrast on the monitor, so that all the lines and characters on the screen are in sharp focus and that the colors are not bleeding around the characters. When the image on the monitor is acceptable, make note of both the brightness and contrast control settings.

Follow the list of possible exposures and take one picture of the screen for each exposure setting. (When doing this, you might set the aperture at f-8 for a better depth of field—i.e., better focus—while shooting at various shutter speeds.) When you have the slides processed, be sure the lab numbers each slide according to the order in which they were taken. This is an easy task that most labs do automatically, since each frame of the slide film is numbered consecutively. If the lab forgets, you can check the number of the slide by carefully separating the slide mount and reading the frame number on the film.

Review your slides in the order they were shot to determine which slide has the quality that you need. Note the number of the slide and check the exposure list to determine the camera settings you used.

Once you have determined the optimal exposure setting, you are ready to shoot your first slide presentation. Create the image using the presentation software package. Adjust the brightness and contrast settings. Then position the camera, set the proper exposure, and start shooting.

There are many factors that may affect the quality of your slides. One of these is room lighting. The face of a computer monitor is glass. Some are manufactured with an antiglare filter that changes the path of the room light after it strikes the monitor. Computer monitors without the antiglare filter give a mirror effect. You can even see your reflection on the screen.

When you are photographing the screen, you should be able to control the lighting in the room. Whenever possible, use a monitor that has an antiglare filter or one that has a low-reflection quality. A high-reflection monitor will pick up even the slightest light in the room and distort the picture.

The only light source you want for the photograph is the computer monitor. All the lighting adjustment is done using the contrast and brightness controls on the monitor—you don't need to use any external lighting. In fact, the best environment to photograph the screen is in a totally darkened room.

The slides you produce with a 35-mm camera will not surpass the quality of slides produced by special photographic equipment designed to capture images from a computer screen. Most of this equipment uses a different approach to photography which is not available to you with your 35-mm camera. However, the quality of the slides you take with your 35-mm camera will be sufficient for most business applications. They will be clear and crisp and well worth the time you spent designing the image and photographing the screen. Remember, however, that this process takes several hours of practice before it can be mastered. And, as always, the best way to learn is through trial and error.

Special Cameras Do the Job

If you can dedicate yourself to mastering the technique of photographing the screen with a 35-mm camera, you can produce slides of sufficient quality for a typical business presentation. However, if you don't have the time to learn, you should purchase a monitor camera that is specially designed for the job.

Monitor cameras are connected directly to the computer through the video output; you connect your display monitor to the camera. When you are preparing the art on the computer, the image will appear on the computer display as usual. Most of the cameras we are going to discuss do not have color monitors. Instead, they use internal, high-resolution black and white monitors, and red, green, and blue filters to produce color images. When you press the shutter control, circuitry in the camera electronically separates the colors of your illustration by breaking down the image into its finest components—the pixels. The camera then reconstructs these picture elements on film. The red, green, and blue filters are placed between the camera's monitor and lens when their corresponding color pixels are presented on the screen of the internal monitor. When all

Monitor cameras like the VideoSlide 35 attach directly to the video output of your personal computer, and your monitor is plugged into the video output of the camera. Although you will be able to see the image that is being photographed on your monitor, the camera is actually shooting another monitor that is built in the camera housing.

the colors of your illustration have been superimposed on the film, the camera advances the film. The result is a perfect picture of the screen.

Monitor cameras are designed to handle the problems of photographing a display screen.

The camera shutter speed and the scan of the monitor used in the camera are engineered for perfect coordination. The light and glare problems don't exist because the entire system (monitor and camera) are contained in a sealed housing. Focusing is not a problem either; the proper distance between the monitor and the lens has been fixed as part of the design. Any focusing adjustments to the lens can only be done with the camera housing disassembled. Monitor cameras are not designed for the user to focus the lens.

You do have control over the type of 35-mm film you use in the camera and, with some models, limited control over the color filters. Many cameras permit the operator to adjust for contrast (i.e., make the blue shade more intense). With some cameras you can even add color to a black and white illustration. You might need this feature if you have three sets of data plotted on a monochrome monitor. With this type of illustration it is easy for the viewer to become lost in the tangle of lines on the screen.

To add color during the filming process, you first have to dissect the graph and reproduce each plotted line separately on the screen. When the first line appears, activate one of the camera's filters (red, green, or blue) and expose this line to the film. Continue this process with the other two lines, changing the color filter.

When you are finished reconstructing the image, all three lines will be on the same piece of film in different colors. Not all cameras allow the operator to override the automatic filtering process. If you are looking for this feature, check to make sure it is available before you purchase the equipment.

Although special cameras take the guesswork out of photographing the computer screen, there are some limitations. When you use a 35-mm camera to capture the image, you have total control over framing the picture. You can move the camera back to capture more of the illustration or focus in on just a segment of the screen. This is useful if the image on the screen contains several different pieces of information that you want to reveal piece by piece as the presentation progresses. You could reproduce enlarged illustrations of each segment, but this will take time. Photographing parts of the screen is more economical.

However, you cannot do this with special monitor cameras. They are set in a fixed position within the housing, so you can photograph only the entire screen, or nothing at all. In most situations, this is a minor inconvenience that can be improved by some software packages. Some presentation software packages can isolate an area of the illustration and enlarge it to fill the screen. Once the image is enlarged, the special camera is able to photograph it. The result is a slide that forms part of a more complex illustration.

A physical limitation referred to as the *aspect ratio,* controls the amount of the screen that will appear on the film. For example, a typical monitor for a personal computer has a 3:4 aspect ratio. This means that for every three pixels on the vertical axis there are four pixels on the horizontal axis. Regardless of the resolution of the monitor, the ratio remains the same.

When filming a subject, it is important that the full frame of the film is filled with the image. On a regular 35-mm camera you are able to adjust the camera to frame the shot properly. In most special cameras designed to photograph the screen, you cannot make this type of adjustment. You must therefore rely on the aspect ratios of the monitor contained inside the camera and of the 35-mm film used to produce the slides.

Unlike the typical monitor, a frame of 35-mm film has an aspect ratio of 2:3. The aspect ratio of the film and that of the monitor do not match. Therefore, the image that appears on the monitor will *not* fit exactly within the frame of film. This slight difference will normally not interfere with the quality of the slide that is produced, although it is a factor to check when you first receive the finished slides. The problem exists even if you switch to a larger-format film such as a 4 × 5 (inch). In this case the aspect ratio is 4:5 and still not a match.

A Closer Look at Special Cameras

The special monitor cameras that take the effort out of photographing the monitor come in a variety of shapes that offer unique features. There are several factors you can use to compare monitor cameras: the variety of adjustment controls available to the operator, how the camera interfaces with the computer, and an assortment of automatic features.

There are three types of adjustment controls you should expect to find on a monitor camera: for brightness, contrast, and chroma. The chroma adjustment permits you to tailor the intensity of the basic colors (red, green, and blue) to your desires. The brightness and contrast control features are self-explanatory. All three of these controls are used to balance the appearance of the slide as it compares to the image on the computer screen. Although in many situations you want to match the slide with the image on the screen, the controls enable you to go a step further and improve on the colors.

It is important to know how the camera interfaces with your personal computer. Some monitor cameras will take either a RGB (red, green, blue) or a composite video feed from the computer, while others will only accept an RGB input. Still other cameras have no interface at all. You place the camera at the narrow end of a black cone and the opposite end of the cone up to the monitor before snapping the picture. The cone controls the proper distance for the shot and limits the lighting to that available from the monitor. Although this is a crude technique, it produces acceptable slides.

Other features that are helpful when photographing the screen are the automatic wind and rewind of the film. Another interesting feature enables you to create a color slide from a black and white image. Some special features are offered at no additional expense. Other features, such as carriages to hold film other than 35-mm, will cost extra. Although some of these features are valuable, be sure you can use the feature. For example, if you rarely produce any black and white slides using your computer, then there is no need to purchase a "color from black and white" option for the camera. You can purchase a less expensive camera that does not have this feature and you will get the same results.

Many monitor cameras cannot interface directly with the output from the IBM Personal Computer. These cameras require an analog signal (as used by radio and television), while the IBM PC generates a digital signal. Use the VideoSlide 35 camera and the VFR-2000 TL-135 by Celtic Tech with your IBM PC and you will not have difficulty interfacing the camera with the personal computer. Other cameras may require some modification before they can be used with the IBM PC.

Cameras in Detail

Once of the most versatile monitor cameras is *VideoSlide 35*, manufactured by Lang Systems, Inc. VideoSlide 35 is the ideal camera for the executive who just wants to load the film and press the button. With the VideoSlide 35 you don't have to become involved with any complicated adjustments. The camera plugs directly into the RGB output of the computer and the monitor is plugged into the VideoSlide 35.

On the front of this camera there are only two controls: one to turn the power on and off and the other to activate the shutter. To take a picture, you turn the power on and press the shutter switch. It's that simple!

After you see the results of your test prints, you may need to adjust the color. You can do so by rotating the three color wheels on the back panel of the camera. Each wheel adjusts the exposure time of the three color filters (red, green, and blue). Unfortunately, these color control wheels do not offer the capability to fine-tune the adjustment by moving the wheel between increments.

The VideoSlide 35 has a 35-mm camera body built into the housing. The only problem with this is that you can only use 35-mm film, ruling out large-format film. Although the camera will accept any 35-mm film, the manufacturer recommends that you use Ektachrome 200 film. This will produce the best results. However, you can also use Kodachrome and Ektachrome 64 to produce acceptable results.

The viewfinder on the VideoSlide 35 enables you to see the image being photographed. You will be able to see the pattern on the screen, but not the color. The red filter covers the image you see on the viewfinder, giving the entire picture a red tint. The colors will, of course, appear in register on the film after the picture is taken. The red tint appears because the camera has the first filter in position.

The VideoSlide 35 has an automatic film advance as standard equipment, but it does not have an automatic rewind. You must rewind the film manually.

Another excellent monitor camera worth considering is the *Model 5000* from Image Resource. Unlike the Video-Slide 35, the Model 5000 can use a variety of film formats, including 35 mm, 4 × 5, and Polaroid SX-70 film packs. For each film format, however, a special film drive option is required. The special equipment is also available from Image Resource.

One of the nice features of the Model 5000 is that you can add color to black and white graphics with this camera. This is an important feature if you are using software packages that only produce black and white graphics. However, the Model 500 does not come with automatic film advance option and so the film must be advanced manually.

The following chart will give you an overview of the more popular monitor cameras on the market.

SLIDES WHILE YOU WAIT

One of the most interesting cameras designed to photograph images from a computer monitor is the *Palette* from Polaroid. This monitor camera produces a 35-mm slide from the screen in just 60 seconds. Although you can produce color slides using the Palette, Polaroid has designed the camera so that you can also produce prints in the same amount of time. As with many other monitor cameras, the Polaroid Palette uses a high-resolution black and white monitor located inside the recorder, and red, green, and blue filters to add color to the image on the film.

Monitor Cameras

Product/Company	Film Format	Add Color To B&W	Automatic Wind/Rewind
VFR-2000-TL-135/Celtic Tech	35 mm	yes	yes/yes
Model 635/Dunn Instruments	any	yes	yes/no
Videoprint 5000/Image Resources	35 mm, 4 × 5 Polaroid	yes	no/no
VideoSlide 35/Lang Systems	35 mm	no	yes/no
Model 3000/Matrix Instruments	35 mm, SX-70 4 × 5, 8 × 10, 16 mm	yes	yes/no
Model MFR-8/Modgraph	35 mm, 4 × 5, SX-70 PR-10, 8 × 10	no	yes/no
Palette/Polaroid	35 mm, 3¼ × 4¼	yes	yes/no

With this camera setup you receive a slide film processor, a device called a recorder (a box in which the image is photographed), and two cameras—a Minolta 35-mm camera for producing slides and a Polaroid Land camera for taking instant pictures (price: around $1500). Also included in the package are all the necessary cables and miscellaneous material needed to develop and mount the slides. All you have to supply are the personal computer, a serial port, and a color graphics board. Of course, you'll also need film.

There are some drawbacks, however. To get the camera up and running, you'll have to refer quite frequently to the documentation that comes with the Palette. There are numerous cables that have to be connected between the camera and the computer, and then there are the normal difficulties one experiences when loading film and switching between the Minolta and the Polaroid Land camera. Furthermore, when you go to check the image through the viewfinder of the Polaroid Land camera, the image will be reversed and upside down.

The cameras that come with the Polaroid Palette can use several kinds of film. Although the manufacturer recommends that Polacolor Type 669 be used for instant prints and Polachrome 35 mm for slides, you can also use Ektachrome, Agfachrome, and Fujichrome. One drawback when you want to snap a picture quickly of the screen is warmup time. Your personal computer may be ready for the shot, but the Palette recorder takes about 20 minutes before it is ready to photograph the screen.

The Polaroid Palette is supplied with software that controls the communication between the camera and your personal computer. The software also enables you to control some of the functions that are available with the Polaroid Palette. This is not a business graphics software package; its only purpose is to facilitate the communication from the computer to the camera and let the operator have limited control over the filming process. When you first boot the Palette software, prepare to spend about an hour to configure the software to your computer. The Palette software is menu driven, which makes it easy to set up the software in conjunction with your computer.

The manufacturer also suggests that you make several test prints. Besides being a good way of learning to use the camera, the test prints enable you to determine if any adjustments to the camera should be made.

When the software is configured, you are instructed to make two key prints: the color key and the color sets. The color key is a print that shows all of the 72 colors that can be produced by the Palette. These colors can be used by the operator to recolor any image that appears on the screen. The color sets print also shows a series of colors that can be called upon to replace any of the colors that appear on the screen. There are eight color sets, each consisting of three colors.

According to the manufacturer, Polaroid Palette can be used with many of the business graphics software packages that are available, including BPS Business Graphics, Chartman, Chart-Master, EnerGraphics, Fast Graphs, Graphmagic, Lotus 1-2-3, Mirrorgraph, PFS:Graph, SignMaster and Visitrend/Plot

Another monitor camera which will give you an instant picture from the monitor is the *Instagraphic* camera from Kodak. Although this is an inexpensive camera and is extremely easy to use, you cannot produce slides with this machine—only instant prints.

The Instagraphic camera comes equipped with a detachable Kodak instant camera and a long, cone-shaped hood. The camera connects to the small end of the cone and is anchored into position using a thumbscrew. After you bring up the image on the monitor, you place the wide end of the cone against the face of the monitor and shoot. You cannot use a tripod with the camera, so you must hold the Instagraphic camera still. This isn't difficult, since part of the cone is resting on the monitor. When you press the shutter button, the built-in film advance mechanism will slide the un-

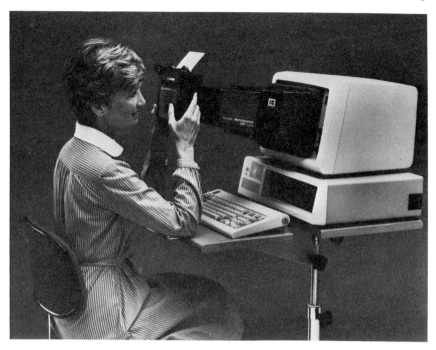

Kodak's Instagraphic monitor camera is a fast and easy way to capture the image on your monitor. The Instagraphic is held against the front of the monitor while you photograph the image.

processed picture from the bottom of the camera. Like other Kodak instant-camera film, you simply place the picture on a table and watch the image appear. Within several minutes you will have an excellent color reproduction of the screen.

The Instagraphic works well, but you will have to use a couple of packets of film before you master it. Special care must be given to framing the picture. If the camera is not centered on the screen, the photograph will be unusable. With a price tag of approximately $200 (compared with the Polaroid Palette selling price of about $1500), the Instagraphic camera is a good unit to keep on hand. Even if the prints turn out to be unusable, in an emergency they can still be used as representative art from which an artist can generate the finished slide.

Which Method Is for You?

Which method is the right one for you? Taking a picture of the screen using a 35-mm camera gives you full control over the entire photographic process. You determine the type of film that is appropriate for the situation. You adjust the shutter speed and aperture opening that control the amount of light that enters the lens when the shutter opens. The flexibility of using a 35-mm camera is especially advantageous if your corporation has a photographer on staff. It shouldn't take the photographer long to master the technique of filming the computer monitor. If you enjoy photography as a hobby and have the time to devote to mastering this photographic technique, then this method is perfect for you. Using a 35-mm camera to photograph the screen of your monitor is usually less expensive than purchasing special photographic equipment. The 35-mm camera costs a few hundred dollars compared with the several thousand dollars you will have to pay for special camera equipment.

Remember, the major drawback of using existing 35-mm equipment to capture the image on your computer monitor is continuity of the output. Because of the scan, the reflection of room lights, glare from the screen, and other factors associated with photographing the screen, conditions change with each session. Adjustments made to the camera, monitor, and the room may not be easy for the photographer to reproduce every time a slide is needed.

The purchase of special photographic equipment is justified when many slides have to be produced within a short period, when there is not time available to reschedule a photographic session, and when no one in the company is familiar with photographic equipment. For most companies that have a constant demand for high-quality presentation slides, the purchase of this equipment is a justifiable expense.

Can you justify the purchase of this equipment? You can determine whether such photographic equipment will be economical by performing a little math. Based on your past experience, estimate the number of slides that your company requires each year, determining the total cost of the material necessary to produce the slide using the personal computer. Include the price of the personal computer, the business graphics software, the special photographic equipment, and the cost of film and processing. Also include the value of the time assigned to the individual who would be operating the equipment. Depending on the approach you use, you may want to spread the cost of the equipment over its entire life span. Divide the total cost by the estimated number of slides you will need. Comparing this amount to the cost you are presently paying for each slide indicates which is more economical.

Keep in mind that there are other noneconomical factors that should be considered before you make a final decision. Factors like turnaround time and creative output, for example, are difficult to quantify but have a critical impact on the outcome.

If you decide to purchase special photographic equipment, visit your local computer dealer and see a number of monitor cameras in operation. You may have to call several dealers before you find one who can demonstrate the equipment. If you are near a major corporate center, look for a dealer who sells only to larger businesses, since the equipment you are looking for is designed for substantial organizations.

Your local computer dealer may not have special photographic equipment on display. In most cases, the dealer will show you a picture of the equipment from a sales brochure and offer to order the product for you—something you can probably do yourself. If a demo unit is not available, you or your dealer should ask the manufacturer of the unit for the name of a customer in your area who is using a similar piece of equipment. The manufacturer may even be willing to arrange a visit with the customer so you can see the unit in operation. If not, go ahead and make the arrangements yourself. Most executives are willing to discuss their experience with a new piece of equipment.

Whether you decide to use a 35-mm camera or special photograhic equipment to capture the image on your computer screen, you will find the photographic method outperforms producing illustrations in hard copy. Once you have mastered the photographic technique, you can reproduce the image on the screen with a flick of the shutter button on the camera.

After processing is completed (some special photographic equipment even has built-in processing for slides), the slide is ready to be used in your presentation. With the proper equipment, this entire process can take less than 15 minutes once you have created the image on the screen. Using a camera eliminates the need for a dot matrix printer or a plotter for producing hard-copy business graphics. Photographing the screen is in many cases (when processing is included with the equipment) a one-step process.

4

Designing a Report Using Business Graphics—A Step-by-Step Approach

Dᴜʀɪɴɢ ᴀ typical workweek, you are often called on to communicate in writing with colleagues. Although most of this communication is routine, both the organization of the material and the presentation are critical to the way the reader perceives you.

The combination of word processing and business graphics software gives you the tools to produce logically organized and dramatic material. We will first show you how this can work for you by using the popular business software series called *PFS*. PFS, published by Software Publishing Corporation, consists of four separate, interactive software packages, PFS:File, PFS:Report, PFS:Graph, and PFS:Write. When used together, they will give you the same capability of using integrated software. Later in the chapter, we turn to the latest integrated software, Symphony and Framework, that you can use to meld text, numbers, and graphs into successful business reports.

The PFS Series

PFS:File is a simple personal filing system with which you can create forms on the screen. These forms can be recalled to the screen and filled in by the operator. The software then stores the completed form on disk for further reference. For example, you can use PFS:File to keep track of regional sales information. Each time a region reports in, that information can be typed into a form generated by PFS:File.

Besides storing information on a disk, PFS:File also gives you the capability to sort and organize the information that has been stored on this computerized file. You can have the software and the computer sort through all of the information on the various forms to produce just the list you want.

Once your information has been stored on the disk using PFS:File, you can use *PFS:Report* to search through the numerical data and, where necessary, perform calculations. You can, for example, have PFS:Report sift through all those regional reporting forms for the gross income and gross profit data. After you make the necessary selection, PFS:Report will determine which percentage of gross income is gross profit. Finally, it will also sort through all the gross profit calculations to find which regions did not achieve their objectives. (You must key the objectives into the software.)

PFS:Report will either display on the monitor or send to the printer just those regions that require priority attention from you. All of the tabular data and calculations can be printed by using PFS:Report.

PFS:Graph will take this numerical information and transform it into business graphics. It can produce line, bar, and pie charts in minutes. Although the art produced by PFS:Graph cannot compare with business graphics software such as ExecuVision and EnerGraphics, the output from PFS:Graph is sufficient to give you a clear picture of the numbers. The graph can be seen on the monitor or printed using a dot matrix printer or a plotter.

For normal daily activities the PFS software that you will use most frequently is *PFS:Write,* a word processing software package. With it, your personal computer is transformed into an electronic typewriter. Since the whole family of FPS software interacts with each other, you can include any of the information produced by the other software package into your document written with PFS:Write.

You can prepare a memo using PFS:Write and indicate (according to steps outlined in the PFS:Write documentation) where a table (created by PFS:Report) or a graph (created by PFS:Graph) should appear in the memo. When the memo is printed, the software will print your text (generated by PFS:Write). It will then stop and locate and print the table and/or graph. PFS:Write will then continue printing the rest of the text.

When you see a memo produced by the PFS series of software, you will notice that text, tables, and graphs all appear on the same page (assuming there is sufficient room). Some other software packages, unlike the PFS series, only offer a single function (word processing, a file system, or a graphics package) and cannot interface. The result is that the text of your memo will be printed on separate pages from the tables and charts. This breaks up the continuity of the thought and creates a less than professional appearance.

Even with the proper tools (computer and software), it is up to you to organize your thoughts and know-how to communicate in writing to a colleague. Writing a good memo or report takes careful planning to assure that the reader understands. Although many executives feel comfortable presenting their opinions over lunch or among a few of their colleagues seated in a conference room, the opportunity for such meetings are rare due to conflicting schedules.

A Drive-Through Using the PFS

The PFS series of software is useful in developing and creating professional memos and reports. Although you can perform any of these tasks using word processing programs, PFS enables you to merge data from files created by other software. Instead of retyping a table of data into a memo, as is required with some software, you can tell PFS:Write to copy the information from a data disk and insert it into the memo.

Using the PFS series to produce your sales memo, you first have to create, using PFS:Graph, the graph that depicts regional sales. When the program boots, a menu will appear on the screen listing all the options.

☐ To enter the sales data into the program so it can produce the graph, press the first option on the menu, Get Edit Data. If you are using the IBM PC version of the program, you must press function key 10 (F10) to register the selection with the software.

☐ The program will present a new menu that asks you if you are going to type the data into the computer, use a VisiCalc file (generated by the VisiCalc program), or a PFS file. In some circumstances you will have already entered your data in a spreadsheet program and stored it in a DIF file. Many popular spreadsheet programs create DIF files that can be used with the PFS series.

☐ Assume that the sales data was not stored in the DIF (Data Interchange Format) file. Therefore, select the first item on the menu. At this point the software asks you for the type of graph you want to produce. In this case, you indicate a bar chart. When you are finished with the selection process, press the F10 key. This brings up the data entry screen.

☐ Type in the data for both the vertical and horizontal axes of the chart. If you make a typing mistake, you can move the cursor over the error and make the correction. After the data have been entered, press the F10 key to return to the main menu.

☐ One of the selections on the main menu allows you to display the chart. Immediately after you make this choice, the computer displays the bar chart which it created using the data that you entered. If the bar chart doesn't give the impact you want, you can save the data to a disk. The data can be recalled and you can experiment with one of the other graphs available from PFS:Graph.

☐ When you have settled on the graph that adequately illustrates your thought, you again press the F10 key and return to the main menu.

☐ From the main menu, choose the Get Save option and press the F10 key. This will bring up another menu, which will have the Save Picture option on it. Select this option and the software will ask you for a file name for the illustration. The file name is critical to saving the graph to a floppy disk. Each name has to be different.

If the name is identical to another file already on the floppy disk, the software will erase the existing file and write the new file in its place.

Once the graph has been saved to the floppy disk, you are finished with PFS:Graph. The file containing the graph, however, will be used when you write your memo using PFS:Write.

CREATING AN OUTLINE WITH PFS:WRITE

When the PFS:Write disk boots, the main menu appears on the screen. The selections include Type/Edit, Define Page, Print, Get/Save/Remove, Clear, and Exit.

- ☐ Use the Type/Edit option to create your document.
- ☐ After the selection is made, pressing the F10 key brings up the blank screen ready for you to type the memo. First outline your memo. This is done by typing your thoughts on the screen one at a time. After each item is completed, the return arrow key is pressed twice. This will leave a blank line between each thought.
- ☐ Once the outline is completed, review the items by using the PGUP and PGDN keys to scroll through each page of the outline.
- ☐ The order of the outline can be changed by moving the cursor to the blank line above or below the item that is being moved. The arrow keys handle the cursor movements. Once the cursor is in position, pressing the return arrow key will open up another line in the outline where you can type your new thought.
- ☐ When you have finished inserting your new idea, you can remove any other item from the screen by placing the cursor on each line you want to remove and pressing the up arrow key and the F6 key. You continue this procedure until all of the items are in the proper order.

Although the procedure just described is efficient when working with a short outline, it can become a time-consuming task if your outline is lengthy. PFS:Write, however, has a block editing feature that enables you to move, copy, and remove entire sections of text. The key to using this feature is to identify the beginning and ending characters in the block of text. This is called *labeling* and only takes a few seconds to accomplish. First you move the cursor to the first character in the block and press the F5 key. Then press the return arrow key until the complete block of text is highlighted on the screen.

What if you make a mistake? There is no problem with PFS:Write. To unlabel the block, just press the F5 key. The label will be removed and the highlighted text will once again return to its normal appearance. Once you have correctly labeled the text, you can perform one of the three functions available with this feature—copy, move, or delete.

With PFS:Write, deleted text is not totally erased. The text is temporarily stored in a portion of the computer's memory called the *block buffer*. You can't see it and it will not appear in your document. However, by pressing the F6 key, the block of text will be reinserted into the document at the position of the cursor. The block buffer has limited space and cannot store multiple blocks of text. In most situations only the last block of deleted text remains in the block buffer as long as the other functions (moving and copying) are not used.

You can move a block of text by deleting the block and recalling it to the screen. The text is labeled and then deleted from the screen using the delete key. The cursor is then positioned to the line where the block is to be inserted. Once the cursor is in position, press the F6 key to bring the block of text to the new position.

You can also have PFS:Write copy a block of text. The block must be labeled first. Move the cursor to the new position and press the F6 key to bring a copy of the block to the second location.

COMPLETING THE MEMO OR REPORT WITH PFS:WRITE

When your outline is completed, position the cursor on the blank line below each item and press the return arrow to open blank space for the text of your memo. You can use the various editing capabilities of PFS:Write to make changes in your text. When your memo is completed, use the arrow keys to move the cursor back to the first item in your outline. Press the up arrow key and the F6 key to remove each line of your outline. If many lines were used for each thought in the outline, use the Block Delete function to remove entire blocks of text from the screen.

Continue this process until all of the outline has been deleted from the screen and replaced with paragraphs of the memo. At any time until the memo is printed, you can reenter the document to make any changes that are necessary.

Assume that you want to include a graph that depicts the status of regional sales. The graph was created and saved to a disk using PFS:Graph. Now it's time to recall the graph and make it part of the printed memo.

- ☐ To insert the graph in the memo, position the cursor on the blank line where the text will be broken and the graph inserted.
- ☐ With the cursor in this position, the return arrow key is pressed to open another blank line.
- ☐ On this new line type *GRAPH(the file name)* and press the return arrow key again.
- ☐ The file name that follows the GRAPH command must be typed exactly the way it was when used to store the graph using PFS:Graph. If you misspelled the file name or added or left out blank spaces, the computer will not be able to find the graph.
- ☐ When you are finished with the document, press the escape key. This will remove the memo from the screen and return you to the main menu.

☐ From the main menu, select the Get/Save/Remove function, which will enable you to save the memo to disk.

☐ The computer will then bring up another menu that enables the user either to retrieve, save, or remove a document from a disk. You need the Save Document option.

☐ After the Save Document selection is registered in the computer, the computer asks for the file name. Remember, this file must have a unique name, one that has not been used for any other file on the disk. Entering the name and pressing the F10 key automatically causes the computer to copy the document onto the disk.

☐ With the document saved, press the escape key to return to the main menu. Now select the Print option. When this selection is made, the computer will ask whether you intend to join files together in the document that is to be printed. Joining files means printing portions of one, then portions from another, and finally returning to print the remainder of the first file. Since you will be joining your memo with a graph, respond with a yes.

☐ The screen clears and presents the printer menu. This contains a listing of six printer manufacturers: IBM Graphics, Epson, Okidata, IDS, NEC, and C.Itoh. Although PFS:Write can print a standard document on any printer, it can print a graph as part of a document only if you are using one of the graphics printers on the printer menu.

☐ Once the selection has been made, the computer will begin printing. The printer will print the memo up to the line where the GRAPH command was inserted. At this line, the computer will switch to the graphic file on the disk containing your sales graph and print it. When this is completed, it will continue to print the rest of the memo.

When you are finished printing, you can always return to the document and make changes. Both the memo and the graph remain on the disk. Changes are made by recalling the document to the screen, making the alterations, and saving it back to the disk.

The final product is a memo that contains both text and graphics all on the same page—a professional-looking document to impress your colleagues.

A Close Look at Symphony

The Lotus Development Company has enhanced and combined a spreadsheet program into an integrated software package called *Symphony*. Similar to other integrated software, Symphony has spreadsheet, word processing, database, graphics, and communications programs built into one software package.

Integrated software packages such as Symphony are ideal for business use. Symphony enables you to join the output of these various programs into a single report. For example, the word processing segment of Symphony can be used to outline thoughts for a report. Later you can expand this itemized list of ideas into paragraphs. Data can be entered using the spreadsheet segment of the program. You can use this portion of the program as a stand-alone spreadsheet to enter and manipulate data as the need arises. Segments of the spreadsheet can be designated as input data for the graphic portion of Symphony. The graph that is generated can then be incorporated into the text of the report.

Symphony is not a program you can master in a few hours. It takes time to master the various features that are available on Symphony, but once you know how to use it, you will find it a highly useful software package.

When Symphony is first loaded into the computer, the access menu appears on the screen. This menu consists of two rectangles stacked on top of each other. The first contains the four options—Symphony, PrintGraph, Translate, and Exit—that you access from this menu. The second instructs you to move the pointer (cursor) to your selection and press the RETURN key. If you are confused, it also instructs you to press HELP for more information.

Symphony is the main program. *PrintGraph* enables you to produce a hard copy of a graph. A unique utility program, *Translate* enables you to convert data files from VisiCalc, dBASE-II, and other programs that generate DIF (Data Interchange Format) files for use with Symphony. *Translate* will also reverse the procedure, making Symphony data files accessible to other such programs except Lotus 1-2-3.

As part of the Symphony program, there is a keyboard template that fits over the function keys. The template helps you to remember the labels of the function keys. For example, at any point in the program you can press the F1 function key to bring a help menu to the screen. The program automatically identifies the type of help you need based on the segment of the program that is being used. Other function keys are used for such features as Edit, Justify, Indent, and Erase. Additionally, each function key has a second function, when it is pressed while the ALT key is simultaneously held down. These features include Compose, Center, Split, Zoom, and Draw, among others.

The function keys are not the only method used to enter special program commands. A combination of other keys will produce special results on the screen. For example, holding down the CONTROL key while pressing the left arrow key will cause the cursor to move left.

WRITING THE SYMPHONY REPORT

A key element in Symphony is its word processing program. When you are ready to begin writing your report, you press the TYPE command: the F10 function key, with the ALT key held down. This will open a blank DOC (document) window on the screen. All of the text will be typed into the DOC window.

Symphony's word processing program is similar to other such programs. It lets you enter text as if you were using a typewriter and has such features as word wrap, which eliminates the need to press the RETURN key when the cursor reaches the end of a typed line.

Above the DOC window, indicators help you keep track of your progress. A cursor line locator tells you which line of the document the cursor is on. A cursor character locator tells you the number of the character on the line where the cursor is stationed. There are also indicators to remind you of justification and the spacing of the document when it is printed.

Once you have created a DOC window and have entered text, you can move the cursor around the text by character, word, line, or paragraph. For example, the arrow keys are used to move the cursor one position right, left, up, or down from the cursor's present position. For example, holding down the CTL key and pressing the appropriate left or right arrow key at the same time moves the cursor a complete word to the left or right.

Pressing the END key followed by either the right or left arrow key will move the cursor to the right or left end of the current line of text. Similarly, pressing the END key followed by the up or down arrow key will move the cursor to the preceding or following paragraph, respectively.

The tips previously discussed about outlining a report using a word processing program can easily be implemented using the word processing segment of Symphony. First, outline your thoughts in the DOC window. Between the thoughts, insert lines of text that elaborate the idea you are presenting. Continue this process until you have text beneath each item in your outline. Once the points have been explained in detail, you can delete your original outline from the DOC window, leaving the body of your report.

Symphony makes it easy to delete and change text. The block of text can be as small as one character or as large as the entire document. Using the cursor control keys, you move the cursor to the beginning of the text block. Pressing the F4 function key will bring the Erase mode into operation, and designates the current position of the cursor as the beginning of the text block that is to be erased. As the cursor is moved to the end of the text block by using the arrow keys, the text is highlighted on the screen. When you reach the end of the text that is to be erased, press the return arrow key to remove the text block from the DOC window.

Symphony enables you to shift whole paragraphs or parts of paragraphs throughout the document. This software package also features global search and replacement of text. For example, if you discover a typographical error in a name used many times in the report, Symphony will automatically correct the spelling in the name each time the name appears. You only have to make the correction the one time the global search and replacement function appears on the screen.

As an integrated software package, Symphony enables you to combine spreadsheet data with word processing text. You can prepare and save your spreadsheet, then using a simple command structure, you can indicate in the text where the spreadsheet data are to appear. Symphony handles the details.

Symphony also enables you to convert spreadsheet data into one of the many graphic styles and then combine the graph with text to form your report. Symphony can produce bar graphs, stack bar graphs, line graphs, plotted line graphs, and pie charts.

Within the graphing mode, Symphony has a unique feature called "what if" graphing. Similar to the "what if" capability of spreadsheets, "what if" graphing depicts the "what if" values in a projected graph. This is ideal for quick comparisons of data.

Symphony offers a wide variety of features and programs that are useful when you must frequently produce reports and give presentations. Symphony is top-of-the-line software that can quickly become a valuable asset to any executive.

A Drive-Through Using Framework

Framework is an integrated software package from Ashton-Tate that offers word processing, database, spreadsheet, business graphics, and an outline feature and communications software. Files generated by one segment of the program can be directly used with any of the other segments.

When Framework is first loaded into the computer, it presents a rectangle that fills the screen. This rectangle, called a *desk* is where you manipulate data, make notes, and use the software to conduct business. At the top of the desk are nine words, called the menu bar. These words are: *Disk, Create, Edit, Locate, Frames, Words, Numbers, Graphs,* and *Prints.* Each of these words is a heading for a submenu that you use to implement the various functions of Framework. For example, when developing a report using Framework, the first task is to create an outline of the report. Framework offers a special feature that is designed to help you organize your thoughts.

Begin by pressing the INS key on the computer. Although IBM calls this the *insert key,* Framework has renamed it the *instruction key.* When the INS key is pressed, the menu bar is activated and the first word on the bar (Disk) is highlighted in reverse type.

Moving the right or left arrow keys enables you to highlight the other words along the menu bar. When the key word on the menu bar is highlighted, the corresponding submenu appears in the upper left corner of the screen. Move the up or down arrow keys to highlight the menu item. Press the return arrow key to activate the selected feature on the menu.

You will want to use the outline feature of Framework to help organize your thoughts for the report. After activating the menu bar by pressing the INS key, move the right arrow key until the word *Create* is highlighted on the menu. Once this appears on the screen, a list of features that are available on the Words submenu will also appear. The Words submenu contain such options as Outline, Empty/Word

Frame, Spreadsheet, Database, Width, Height, Columns/Fields, and Rows/Records. You will be using the Outline feature. Empty/Word Frame is used for word processing, and Spreadsheet and Database are self-explanatory. The remaining categories are used to define the spreadsheet and database programs.

Move the down arrow until the word *Outline* is highlighted and then press the return arrow key. The submenu is removed from the screen and is replaced by a larger framed area on the "desk." Although the framed area fills up most of the screen, you can still see the menu bar at the top of the screen and a message line at the bottom of the screen. Also on the screen, in the upper right corner, is a clock and a disk drive indicator that highlights which drive is in use.

All of your work will be done within the frame. (By now you're getting to know why this software package is called Framework.) While we are in the Outline frame, the computer has already set up the basic structure for your outline. There are three major topics, which are numbered 1, 2, and 3 and are flagged with an arrowhead beside the number. Below and slightly to the right of the major topic headings are three subtopic headings, which are indicated by 1.1, 1.2, and 1.3. The first number corresponds to the major topic while the second number indicates the order of the subtopic.

Framework Outline

```
1
    1.1
    1.2
    1.3
2
    2.1
    2.2
    2.3
```

```
3
   3.1
   3.2
   3.3
```

Although Framework starts you off with only three major topics and three subtopics, you can easily increase the number by adding topics and subtopics to the list. Framework also enables you to change any of the ideas in the outline.

☐ To begin the outline, press the DOWN LEVEL key. (This is the plus-sign key on the key pad. The minus key on the key pad is the UP LEVEL key.) When the Down Level key is pressed, the highlighted area moves inside the frame to the first major topic of the outline

☐ Type the first major idea you want to cover in your report. For example, if the report will cover the introduction of a new product, the first topic might be called Manufacturing. This would be typed next to the heading on the outline.

```
1 Manufacturing
   1.1
   1.2
   1.3
2
   2.1
   2.2
   2.3
3
   3.1
   3.2
   3.3
```

☐ After you have identified the first topic of the outline, press the TAB key to move the highlighted area to the first subtopic under Manufacturing. Following the same procedure, type in the first subtopic under Manufacturing. In this case it will be called Suppliers.

1 Manufacturing
   1.1 Suppliers
   1.2
   1.3
2
   2.1
   2.2
   2.3
3
   3.1
   3.2
   3.3

☐ Repeat this process until you have completed your outline.

1 Manufacturing
   1.1 Suppliers
   1.2 Assembly
   1.3 Distribution
2 Advertising
   2.1 Target Audiences
   2.2 Advertising Campaign
   2.3 Advertising Expenses
3 Sales
   3.1 Sales Organization
   3.2 Sales Strategy
   3.3 Sales Forecast

Although the TAB key helps to move you quickly through the first round of work on your outline, you need more flexibility. You can get it through Framework's special-function keys. For example, pressing the up and left arrow keys at the same time will move the highlighted area up one item. The down and right arrow keys pressed together will move you down to the next item. You can use the HOME key to move to the first item in the outline and the END key to the last item.

To make outline changes, move the highlighted area to the line that needs to be altered. Pressing the space bar will cause the topic or subtopic to appear on the edit line. Once there, you can move the arrow keys to the position where the changes are to be made and then type the new characters over the old characters. If you want to erase a character, position the cursor over the character and press the DEL key. After you have completed your changes, press the return arrow key and the changed topic or subtopic appears in position on the outline.

You can easily save your outline to a disk for future reference and updating. Pressing the CONTROL key together with the return arrow key will cause Framework to automatically save the outline to disk. With the outline saved to the disk, you will want to print a copy of the outline to refer to while you are developing the final report.

□ First, press the UP LEVEL key, which highlights the frame, and then press the INS key, which opens the print menu and highlights the first item on the menu, "Begin."

□ After checking that the printer is ready, press the return arrow key and the outline will print.

KEYING IN THE FRAMEWORK NUMBERS

With the outline in hand, you can now assemble the data that will be used to create the graph for the final report. You will be using Framework's spreadsheet program. Framework's spreadsheet program is a standard spreadsheet. It provides the same basic command structure using the coordinates of columns and rows to identify cells of information.

□ To enter the spreadsheet program, press the UP LEVEL key and then the INS key. This places the highlighted area on the menu bar.

☐ Move the highlight to the Create menu's spreadsheet subselect and press the return arrow key.

☐ The spreadsheet will appear on the screen. By moving the cursor control keys, you can insert headings and data in any of the columns and rows on the spreadsheet. In this case, you want to insert the sales forecast for the next five years. Each year will have its own column. Once you have finished, save the spreadsheet to disk.

CREATING A FRAMEWORK GRAPH

Before you set out to write the final version of your marketing report, you need to create a graphic display of projected sales. The sales data have already been entered into the spreadsheet segment of Framework and have been saved to a disk. Now you want to have Framework develop a graph that will be printed as part of your marketing report.

☐ The first step requires that the CONTROL key and the G key be pressed together. This opens the Graph menu.

☐ To make a graphic presentation of each column, press the C key followed by the D key.

☐ Finally, the return arrow key causes the software to draw the bar graph. The column headings will be the same as those used on the spreadsheet.

Framework allows you to dress up the chart by creating your own titles, which can be placed anywhere on the chart. It can also draw the graph so it fits properly into the space you are working with. Besides a bar chart, Framework can produce stacked bar, pie charts, line graph, and marked points. It can even explode parts of the pie chart.

To incorporate your graph into the printed report, the next step is to label the graph and have the computer recalculate and redraw the graph. (This you accomplish by pressing the F5 function key.) Once you are satisfied with the graph, you must save it to disk. To do this, press the

UP LEVEL key followed by the INS key. Using the arrow key, move the highlighted area to the Disk menu's subselection Put Away and press the return arrow key.

THE FINAL FRAMEWORK REPORT

You will use Framework's word processing program to actually write your report.

- [ ] Once again, press the UP LEVEL key followed by the INS key. This places the highlighted area on the menu bar.
- [ ] Using the arrow keys, move the highlight to Create.
- [ ] With the down arrow key highlight Empty/Word Frame, which is the selection following Outline.
- [ ] A blank frame appears on the screen. This is the area where you will write the report. Framework's word processing program is very similar to others that are on the market. You type your report as if you were using a typewriter. The control keys enable you to insert and delete text and perform all the standard functions.

The report will be divided into three frames. The first frame will contain text up to the portion of the program where you want the graph to be inserted. The second frame contains the graph, and the third frame contains the remaining text. Finally, all three frames will be contained in an empty frame.

- [ ] Move the highlight to the menu bar and select the Create menu. Within this menu, select the Empty/Word Frame submenu and press RETURN. This will open an empty frame on the screen. This frame must be labeled.
- [ ] Press the DOWN LEVEL key. This will move the cursor inside the empty frame.

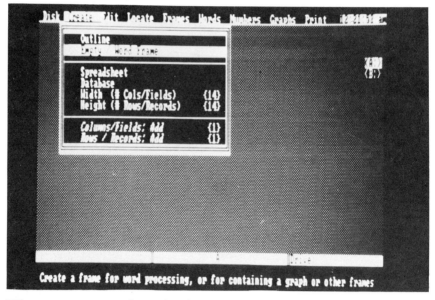

When you are ready to begin writing a document using Framework, select the Create option that opens the Create submenu. Here you can select Empty/Word Frame.

☐ Again return to the Create menu and select Empty/Word Frame. This will place another empty word frame within the one already on the screen. This should be labeled as the first portion of your text.

☐ Follow the same procedure until the other frames of the report are labeled.

After you have followed the outline and prepared the marketing report, you must return to the document and enter formatting and printing commands. These are the special codes that set the printing margins, the length of a page, and other information that is required to print the document.

☐ Once you are ready to print, press the F10 function key to view each frame within the containing frame.

KEY	MOVES THE CURSOR	KEY	MOVES THE CURSOR
UPLEVEL (Gray −)	to the border of a frame	DOWNLEVEL (Gray +)	into a frame from its border
←	back one character	Ctrl ←	back one word
→	forward one character	Ctrl →	forward one word
↑	up one line	Ctrl ↑	back one sentence
↓	down one line	Ctrl ↓	forward one sentence
Home	to beginning of line	Ctrl Home	to beginning of frame
End	to end of line	Ctrl End	to end of frame
PgUp	top of page, then back a frameful	Ctrl PgUp	back one paragraph
PgDn	page bottom, then ahead a frameful	Ctrl PgDn	ahead one paragraph

Previous Screen   Next Screen   Index of Topics   Key Help
Select an option with ← or → and press RETURN; press ESC to exit

Typing a document using Framework is similar to using any word processing program. Special keys enable you to move the cursor around the screen among the functions. If you need help, Framework will show you a screen that lists all the commands you need to enter text.

☐ When you are satisfied with the arrangement of the frames, press the UP LEVEL key followed by the INS key.

☐ Then move the highlighted area to the print menu using the arrow keys.

☐ Press the return arrow key and the computer will print the report.

As long as you have saved all of the segments of the report on disk, you can always go back into your disk file and make alterations without any difficulties. The computer will automatically redraw the graph and reprint a revised report for you.

5

Designing Microcomputer Art for Your Slide Presentation—A Step-by-Step Approach

We have discussed the finer points of preparing a meeting in the introduction. In this chapter we will concentrate on how to use business graphics software to enhance your presentation.

Planning the Visuals

With your speech in hand, you can begin to work on your slides for the presentation. Slides have two major purposes: to entertain the audience visually and to highlight dramatically the points made by the speaker. The entertainment value can be put to good use in title slides that grab the audience's attention as your presentation begins. Such slides might show the company logo or the name of the project being presented. In contrast, an informational slide graphically compares two or more items that are being discussed. Pie charts and bar graphs are examples of informational slides.

When you design your slides, remember that they should be kept simple and easy to understand in order to enhance your presentation. For example, you might use a bar chart to illustrate the dramatic growth in sales over a five-year period. The slide should give the audience a quick visual impression of the sales figures: a graduated scale in dollars on the vertical axis and the years under each bar on the horizontal axis. The slide should also be titled. Any other piece of information on the slide might clutter it and detract from its true purpose—to support the facts being presented by the speaker. Related information—such as yearly percentage increases in sales—should be presented orally or on a separate slide.

As you prepare your speech, it will be obvious where slides are needed to enhance the presentation. A pattern usually develops where a slide is required for each 15 to 20 seconds of the speech. The life of a slide on the screen is relatively short. For simple title slides, the audience will become bored by looking at it for five seconds. More complex slides, such as bar charts, have a slightly longer life, since it takes the audience more time to digest the information contained on the slide.

The first step in determining the visual aspect of the presentation is for you to read the script and note where the text discusses critical points. It isn't important at this stage to decide the type of slide to use. This will come in the second draft of the visual presentation.

In most presentations, you will need an opening or title slide as well as a number of slides to illustrate each point in the presentation. Also include the title slides in the visual portion of the script, even though these slides may not be directly associated with a fact in the script. After analyzing where slides are needed, you should have your assistant add this information to the script to produce a second draft on the visual portion of the script. Now you can concentrate on the style of the slides that are to be used.

At this point you will determine if a bar chart or a pie chart should be employed. Should the slides build on each other, for example, by starting with one bar on a chart and then after three slides ending up with five bars on the same slide? There are a few guidelines you can follow that will help you communicate better with your audience.

GUIDELINES FOR YOUR VISUALS

If you are presenting a multisegment plan such as "Five Steps that Will Increase Sales," you should use a series of index slides throughout the presentation. An index slide lists the five segments that are to be discussed. The first slide, for example, highlights all five segments. As you begin talking about each segment, an index slide appears, highlighting only the segment being discussed. A series of index slides gives the audience a reference point during the speech to help them know when the discussion will move to the next segment.

You should avoid using any slides that depict a spreadsheet of numbers. In most cases, the audience will not be in the position to study carefully the material in the slide. The information will therefore be lost. In place of a screen filled with numbers, you should use charts and graphs to enhance your presentation. These are easier for the audience to digest quickly.

It is a good idea to reserve all details of a presentation to documentation handed out to the audience after the presentation has concluded. This is especially important when you expect your colleagues to implement the plan or project under discussion. For example, a presentation introducing a new sales strategy should discuss the strategy in general terms. Later, you can meet individually with each executive to discuss those details that affect him or her. It is disruptive to have 10 regional managers in the room while you cover in detail how the strategy is going to affect just one of those managers. The material you present must be of interest to *everyone* in the room.

Keep the size of the slide and the style of the illustration on the slide consistent throughout the presentation. For example, if you use 24-point type for a headline on a slide, use the same size for the headlines on all the slides. Keeping the same style on all the slides will give the slide presentation a professional appearance.

Use slides with dramatic, complicated illustrations only if the illustrations are of professional quality. Although you can use a variety of business graphics software packages like ExecuVision to create flags, maps, and nearly anything your imagination can dream up, you still must have the artistic capability to draw those images. Some software such as ExecuVision have clip-art libraries available for use with their programs. Clip-art illustrations are prepared by a professional artist and stored on a disk so you can incorporate the illustrations into your own slide.

When clip art is available, use it. The results will dramatize your presentation and give it a truly professional appearance that will impress your audience. If clip art is not available, and you don't have the artistic talent available to create your own illustrations, then keep your slides simple.

The slides will be less dramatic but will still give that professional appearance you need.

Alongside the text of the second draft, make a rough drawing of the slides that will be used to highlight each segment of the speech. These drawings will help you to judge whether they are appropriate for the presentation. As you continue to review the speech, you will find it easier to visualize the slides that will be used in the presentation. Once you are satisfied with the order of the slides, you can prepare the details of each illustration. Detailed drawings of each slide should be prepared on 8 1/2 × 11-inch paper. Make the mock-up as accurate as possible. The detailed illustration should contain all the components of the slide as they will appear on the slide. Since some business graphics software packages will create charts and graphics from raw data, you should include as part of your preparation the numeric data that are to be depicted on the slide.

Rehearsing Your Presentation

With the large detailed drawings of the slides prepared, you should assemble the drawings in order of appearance. A couple of close associates should be invited to hear you rehearse your presentation. While timing the speech, you should read it aloud and display the drawings of the slides in the appropriate order. Although this initial rehearsal will lack the polish of a finished presentation, it should be sufficient for your colleagues to indicate where improvements are necessary. You should give their objective remarks serious consideration when revising the presentation.

When the script has been polished and the slides have been prepared, you should rehearse the entire presentation. During this practice run, you should indicate on the script when the slides should be shown. These slide cues should appear on every copy of the script. In some situations, for example, you might ask another person to advance the slides.

This person will require a complete script (audio and video) including the slide cues.

The rehearsal should consist of the complete presentation. All the slides should be shown to assure that they are of good quality and can be comfortably seen by everyone in the audience. If several people are going to speak, you should verify that each presenter's segment is of the proper length. You must judge if the points made by the presenters can be clearly understood. If each presenter has followed the guidelines discussed in this chapter, the rehearsal of the presentation should run smoothly and will not require any last-minute adjustments except for minor alterations of the audiovisual equipment.

Handouts

In most instances, your audience will forget most of what was presented within the first two hours following the meeting. Regardless of how well you present your material, the audience will retain only a fraction of your presentation—general themes will be remembered but details will be lost.

It becomes critical in some business situations for the participants in the meeting to remember the facts that were presented. Regional managers, for example, whose job it is to carry out the new marketing strategy, must retain sufficient details to follow through on the plan after the meeting.

To increase the retention of the audience, reinforce the details by using several techniques. The first step is to limit the amount of detail you present to the audience during the meeting. Limit the critical points to one or two facts. After the meeting you can reinforce these points by distributing documentation. These handouts should cover the material that was presented and describe in detail what the participant must know to fulfill the plan. The participant can read through the handout material several times and retain more of the information with each reading.

Handouts should contain all of the "how to" information such as what the colleague's role will be in the plan, who should be contacted for further instruction, what the flow of paperwork is, what the deadlines are, and how the plan works.

Handouts must be well organized and clearly written. They should contain flowcharts and other illustrations that make it easy for the reader to understand the instructions. For example, if the participant is to prepare forms, include samples of those forms already filled out in the handout.

If you use dramatic or complicated slides during the presentation, it will be helpful for the audience if printed copies of those slides are contained in the handout. Although you can eliminate title slides from the handout, charts and graphs should be included.

A week or two after the meeting you should contact each of the participants by phone to ascertain your colleagues' impressions of the meeting and of the material that was presented. You can also elicit feedback that will indicate whether the colleague understood the important points of the presentation. Finally, during the conversation you can again reinforce the details presented during the meeting.

Using ExecuVision

A popular business graphics software package distributed by Prentice Hall, ExecuVision is a state-of-the-art graphics presentation program for executives who frequently are called on to give professional presentations. ExecuVision runs on IBM and IBM-compatible personal computers. ExecuVision combines the maximum graphic capabilities with speed, ease, and versatility. Besides having the capability to produce the usual business graphics such as pie, bar, and line graphs, ExecuVision can produce text and image processing in 35 colors. The stand-alone graph capability can be combined with visually striking animation techniques, color sketching, provocative special effects, and hundreds of professionally rendered clip-art illustrations. All of these are ready to be incorporated in your slide presentation.

ExecuVision's painting feature transforms your computer monitor into an artist's canvas. You have complete control over the style of brush and color and the size of various typefaces that are to be used. You can electronically cut and paste, move, or remove any element in the slide. All of this is achieved using menus. The software uses simple keyboard interface to allow you to control the creation of the slide. There is no need for joysticks or paddles to produce the illustration. ExecuVision is completely menu driven. On-screen features explain each menu option and function.

ExecuVision also offers 10 different styles of type that can be used in the slide. Each of these styles can be automatically increased or decreased in size depending on your requirements.

When ExecuVision first boots, the main menu appears on the screen consisting of five options: Create, Prepare, Print, Run, and Quit. The arrow keys enable you to move the cursor to the option you desire, while the return arrow key brings up the option to the screen.

To develop your slide, select the Create option. Pressing the return arrow key brings the Create menu to the screen. The options are: Object, Text, Cut, Save, Motion, New, Tools, Sketch, Color, Load, Dump, and Exit. Place the cursor on the Text selection and press the return arrow key.

There are only three items on the text menu: Begin, Font, and Exit. Although you can select the Begin option, which will enable you to enter text to your slide, select the Font option first. The Font option enables you to select the style of type you want to use for your slide. Selecting the Font option brings to the screen yet another menu, one that lists the styles of font that are available. These include Futura, Singdot, Italic, Data, System, and Block1. Another option calls up an additional font menu containing styles such as Euros1, Block2, Euros2, and Bold. To appreciate the various styles that are available, you should experiment with ExecuVision. When you make your selection, the name of the font you select appears on the screen along with the size of the type. The size is indicated by "W 14 H 10," or 14 pixels wide and 10 pixels high. After you have made your selection, the Text menu reappears on the screen with the cursor at the Begin option. When you press the return arrow key, the program will enable you to type text onto your slide.

The cursor will appear in the center of the screen. By moving the arrow keys you can position the cursor anywhere on the screen. Position the cursor in the screen location where the first word is to begin. Start typing. The text will appear in the font you selected. If you make a mistake, you can move the cursor, using the arrow keys, to the mistake and retype it. When you are finished typing, press the return arrow key. This will bring the Create menu to the screen again. Before you continue to enhance your slide, it is advisable to save the slide to disk. Save is an option on the Create menu. After selecting it, the program will ask you to name the slide, and the computer saves it for you.

After the slide has been saved, the computer will return you to the Create menu again. Select Text and press the return arrow key to bring up the second Create menu (Begin, Font, Exit). Now select Begin. ExecuVision enables you to type in a number of colors by pressing the F9 function key. For example, when you press the F9 key the first time, the cursor turns light blue. Anything you type will appear in this color. Hit the F9 key once more and the cursor color changes to purple. If you had typed when the cursor was light blue, the characters would have remained that color. Only the new text will be in the second color. The third and fourth colors are gray and black. These are also activated by pressing the F9 key. ExecuVision enables you to use a set of four colors at a time. This is called a palette. There are three more palettes available in a variety of colors that broaden your creative capability with this software. The second palette consists of cyan, magenta, white, and black. The third palette offers pine green, red, brown, and black. The final palette contains green, rose, yellow, and black.

One of the interesting features of ExecuVision is its ability to let you sketch your own illustrations onto the slide. When the cursor is positioned on the Create menu, select the sketch feature by placing the cursor on the selection and pressing the return arrow key. One of the more common uses of the sketch feature is to underline text or to draw a border around the slide. Once the sketch selection has been made, position the cursor where you want to begin to draw. Holding the shift key down while you move the arrow keys will cause the software to light a pixel in the position of the cursor. Releasing the shift key will enable you to move the cursor freely around the screen without leaving a mark. If you make a mistake or want to remove a segment of the sketch from the screen, position the cursor over the area that is to be removed and press the DEL key. The software automatically removes that portion of the sketch from the screen.

ExecuVision enables the artistic executive to increase or decrease the size of the line drawn on the slide. For example, by pressing the ALT key and simultaneously hitting the number *1*, the size of the cursor will become one point thick. (This is the narrowest the cursor can become.) Hit the number *9* and the cursor's thickness becomes nine points, the widest available. Once you have established the size of the cursor, use the arrow keys to position the cursor. Press the shift key in conjunction with the arrow keys to draw the line on the screen the thickness of the cursor.

Now that you have placcd the text on the screen and incorporated your own sketches in the slide, you can also use the clip-art library feature of ExecuVision to give your slide a professional image. If your presentation involves a discussion of personal computers, you can add a professionally sketched illustration of a personal computer on the slide in the position you designate.

USING THE CLIP-ART LIBRARY

☐ Bring up the Create menu and select the Load option. The Load option will produce this submenu on the screen: Slide, Pix, Pixmix, Pixinv, Vplot, Exit.

☐ Select Pix and press the return arrow key. The software asks for the name of the picture. In this case the name of the picture from the clip-art library is *Personal Computer.*

☐ After the name is entered into the computer, the software will prompt you to insert the library disk in drive B.

☐ The software will load the sketch of the personal computer and place it in the center of the screen. The image will blink, indicating that you have an option to leave the illustration in the center of the slide or move it.

☐ Use the arrow keys to move the illustration around the slide. When you have selected the final position of the illustration, press the return arrow key.

ExecuVision has a wide variety of clip-art libraries that you can use to create your own slides. In their Border Collection library, you will find ready-to-use borders such as blackboard, bulletin board, and clipboard. This library also includes fancy borders like skyscrapers, stars and stripes, streamers, and a Wall Street border. Besides the Border Collection library there are Maps and Regions, Health and Fitness, Financial Services, Transportation, Computers and Computer Applications, Initials and Decorative Designs, Industry and Business, and Professionals: The World's Faces and Figures. Each of the libraries contains hundreds of possible picture combinations that will enable you to create dynamic, individualized visual presentations.

In the Maps and Regions library you will find maps of almost every part of the world, to which you can add your own words and figures. This is especially useful when presenting regional sales information. ExecuVision actually en-

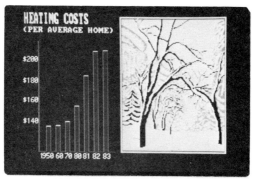

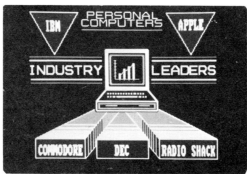

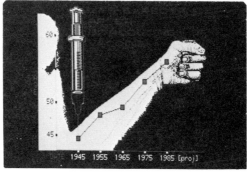

Created using ExecuVision. Originals in full color.

ables you to show the region in the slide. In the Industry and Business collection, for example, there are detailed sketches of factories, office buildings, and of products associated with manufacturing and business.

SCALING THE TEXT

One of the most interesting features provided by Execu-Vision is scaling. This feature enables you to change the size of the text to add more drama to the slide. Before you begin to type the text on the slide, you can increase or decrease the size of the text cursor just as you adjusted the cursor in the sketch segment of the program.

☐ First press the F1 function key, which will place the program in the Scale mode.

☐ While holding down the shift key, you can change the size of the cursor by moving the arrow keys. The up and/or right arrow keys will increase the cursor while the down and/or left arrow keys will decrease it.

☐ With the size of the cursor selected, you press the F2 function key to complete the scaling processing.

☐ Whatever you type after this point will appear in the corresponding size of the cursor. The font, however, will not change; you can use the scaling feature with any font.

ExecuVision can bring new life to any presentation, and it can handle the chores of plotting a graph. The program can produce pie, bar, or line graphs from DIF files or by entering data directly into your personal computer. The graph can then be enhanced using the other creative features offered by ExecuVision.

Although in this chapter we have concentrated on preparing slides for a presentation using a personal computer as a slide generator, ExecuVision—as will be seen in the next chapter—can also turn your personal computer into a slide projector. For example, you can create a series of slides, store them on a disk, and instruct ExecuVision to recall each of them in the proper sequence according to your script. You can animate parts of the slide. ExecuVision has a special animation feature that adds movement to your presentation.

Before you prepare your next slide presentation, be sure you take a few moments to consider the advantages ExecuVision offers you. With this package you will probably present a professional-looking slide show for a fraction of the cost of employing an artist.

Using EnerGraphics

There are times when preparing slides for a presentation when you will require special treatment of data such as advanced statistical analysis used when plotting a graph. Or you might need a slide that contains mechanical drawings or floor plans. The answer to these requirements is a soft-

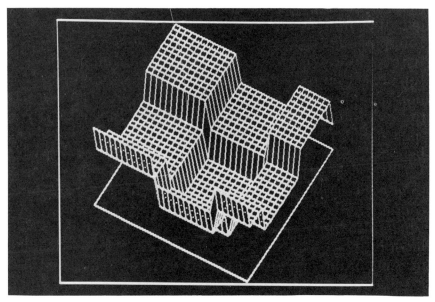

A key element of a business graphics software package like EnerGraphics is its ability to produce three-dimensional illustrations.

ware package called *EnerGraphics* that runs on the IBM PC or PC-compatible computers. EnerGraphics is capable of producing a pie chart with up to 15 slices. It can generate bar charts with negative and multiple scales. EnerGraphics can even stack the graphs and produce three-dimensional charts. When it comes to line charts, this software package can produce charts with up to 10 lines and 200 data points for each line and can use log or semilog scales. It will even generate charts using linear and polynomial regression.

When you combine these advanced statistical features with EnerGraphics' ability to accept data files from VisiCalc, Lotus 1-2-3, and Multiplan, you have a powerful business graphics package that can make it quick and easy to produce a slide for a meeting.

The most interesting features available with Ener-Graphics is its drawing capability. You can produce organizational charts, flowcharts, even develop special logos. EnerGraphics is ideal for producing floor plan layouts,

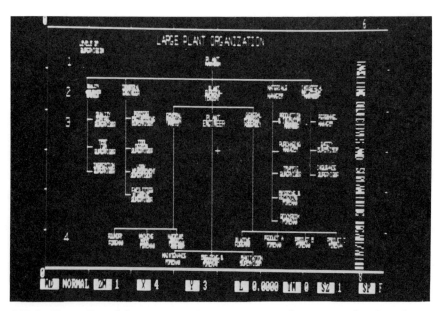

With EnerGraphics you can create complex organizational tables. The symbols used in this table can be created in advance and saved to disk.

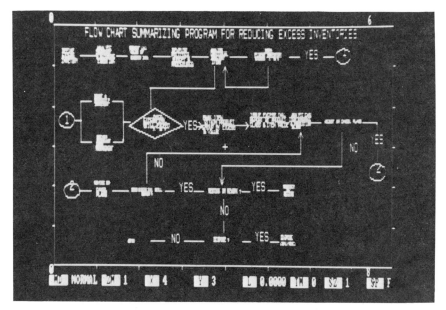

EnerGraphics is an ideal program for designing flowcharts.

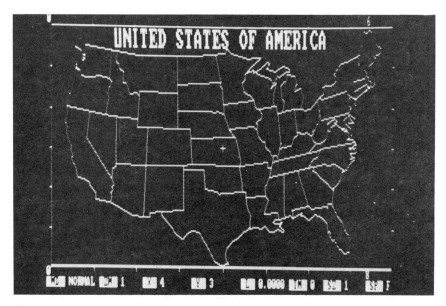

You can use EnerGraphics to design logos and product symbols. Here is an example of how EnerGraphics and an artistic operator can create an illustration that could later be reduced and moved to a slide.

electrical circuit design, mechanical drawings, and architectural drawings and is perfect for developing advertising layouts.

When you produce a three-dimensional chart, Ener-Graphics enables you to zoom in on particular areas of the slide and rotate the slide on the screen. These features cut down the time it takes to produce a series of enlargements that are part of a main slide. For example, you can use the program to generate a three-dimensional chart. Once you have photographed the screen, you can zoom in on an area of the chart to make the second slide in the series. By rotating the chart and zooming in on another area of the chart, you can produce still another slide. All this is possible by having the software produce one chart on the screen.

DRAWING A PIE CHART WITH ENERGRAPHICS

Once EnerGraphics is loaded, the main menu appears on the screen. This contains five items: Charts, 2-D Graphics, 3-D Graphics, Support, and Utilities. The selections are made by pressing the corresponding function keys, F1 through F5. In our first exercise using EnerGraphics we will draw a pie chart.

□ Press the F1 Charts selection from the main menu to bring up the Chart menu to the screen. This lists three options: Pie Charts, Bar Charts, and Line Charts. Use the function keys to select the Pie Chart option.

□ The Pie menu appears on the screen listing nine options: Creat Pie Chart, Draw Pie Chart, Print Pie Chart, Edit Pie Chart, Save Pie Chart, Read Pie Chart, Delete Pie Chart, Show File Directory, and Return to the Main Menu. Since you want to create a pie chart, press the first function key (F1).

□ The screen clears and presents a computerized form for entering the data necessary to generate the pie chart. The first item entered is the name of the chart.

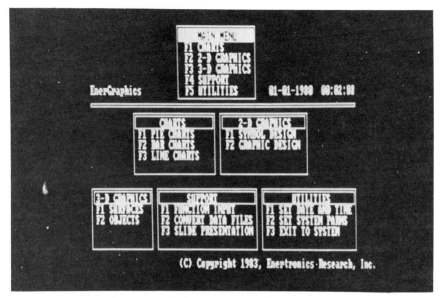

Creating a graph or mechanical drawing with EnerGraphics is easy because every step in the program is menu-driven. For example, when the program is first loaded, the master menu appears, enabling the user to move quickly to the appropriate segment of the program.

☐ After you press the return arrow key, the cursor automatically moves the first slice of the pie down. The software asks you for the numeric value of this slice.

☐ You must also select your colors. EnerGraphics offers two sets of colors—green, red, and yellow or cyan, magenta, and white. These colors are listed by number on the screen. The number of the color is entered next to the numeric value of the slice.

☐ Next, the software needs to know the pattern to be used in the slice. Similar to the color selection, there are three patterns displayed on the screen—no pattern, stripes, and solid. Alongside the patterns are numbers that are used to enter the selection.

☐ The software then wants to know if the slice is to be offset, pulled away from the other slices. A "Y" or "N" is sufficient to indicate your requirements.

☐ You are then asked to type in the description of the slice. Whatever you enter in response to this prompt will appear outside of the pie near the slice.

☐ The process continues until you have entered all the data for the entire pie chart. If a mistake is made during the process, you can use the function key to either insert a slice or delete a slice.

☐ When you are finished press the CONTROL and END keys.

The EnerGraphics software will then display the completed form and ask you if you want to have percentage labels appear inside each slice. If you respond with a "Y," the software will print within each slice the corresponding percentage of the entire pie chart that the slice represents. After this selection you press the return arrow key and the Pie Chart menu will once again appear. As a precaution it is wise to save the pie chart to a disk by pressing the F5 function key. After the chart has been saved, press the F2 function key asking the software to draw the pie chart. The program asks if you want to the chart in low, medium, or high resolution. EnerGraphics refers to low resolution as *medium resolution A*. Medium resolution is referred to as *medium resolution B*. Once the selection is made and the return arrow key pressed, the screen clears and the pie chart is drawn.

Since you intend to photograph and make the image into a slide, it is critical that you select the high-resolution option for all of the pie charts that you generate using EnerGraphics. This high-resolution pie chart will make a better-looking slide.

Pressing any key will return you to the Pie Chart menu. From this menu you can enter any of the other options. For example, you could select Edit to return the data form to the screen to can change any aspect of the pie chart.

CREATING A BAR CHART WITH ENERGRAPHICS

Creating a bar chart is similar to the procedures used in making a pie chart.

☐ From the main menu select the Chart option, which brings up the Chart menu.

☐ Select the Bar Chart option to call up the Bar Chart menu. This menu has the same features that are found on the Pie Chart menu.

☐ To begin, select the Create option. The software first asks if you are going to use a single scale or multiple scales for the bar chart.

☐ Type "S" for single and "M" for multiple. In this example you are going to use multiple scales.

☐ The screen clears and then asks for the title of the chart and the labels used to describe the vertical and horizontal axes.

☐ The screen clears once more and asks for the minimum and maximum scale values and the value of the steps used on the scale. Typically, 0 would be entered as the minimum scale value, 100 as the maximum scale value, and 10 as the value of each step. The scale value will vary with the values used in your data series.

☐ After pressing the return arrow key after each input, the software asks you for a subtitle. The subtitle is the name given to one series of data produced in the bar chart. For example, if the chart is comparing two sets of data, the chart will contain two subtitles.

☐ The software then needs to know where on the chart the subtitle is to be printed. The location is designated by using a grid containing rows from 3 to 23 and columns from 12 to 75. The first character of the subtitle will appear in the coordinate given by the user.

☐ The next piece of information requested by the software is the color and patterns to be used with the bar chart. Selections are made with the same method used with the Pie Chart option.

☐ Finally, the software asks you to enter the data that are to be illustrated by the bar chart.

☐ When you are finished entering this information, press the CONTROL and END keys together.

☐ A submenu appears on the screen giving you the option to press the CONTROL and END keys to complete the chart or to press any other key to create another graph. Since you are going to compare two sets of data, enter the Create a Graph selection.

Once again you are asked to select subtitles, bar patterns, colors, etc. You are also requested to enter the next series of data. When these tasks are completed, pressing the CONTROL and END keys together will cause the software to ask for the labels that will be printed beneath each bar. This is the last request made by the software. After the return arrow key is pressed, the software will return to the Bar Chart menu.

Save the chart to disk and then have the software draw the chart on the screen. The software asks you to select the resolution of the image and whether it will be in two or three dimensions. If two dimensions is selected, the bar will lay flat on the screen. A three-dimensional view will give each bar a boxlike appearance.

The software also needs to know whether you want multiple or stacked bars. Multiple bars show sets of bars alongside each other. Stacked bars show sets of bars on top of each other. It then asks whether the bars should be vertical or horizontal. Finally, it needs to know whether you want horizontal scoring and numbered scales.

After all of the responses have been answered, pressing the return arrow key will cause the program to generate the bar graph on the screen. Like the pie chart, pressing any key will cause the software to bring up the Bar Chart menu.

GENERATING FLOWCHARTS WITH ENERGRAPHICS

EnerGraphics' other charts and graphs are generated using the same procedures used in producing the pie and bar charts. EnerGraphics can also be used to generate flow-charts and similar designs. The objective of this example is to show you how to create symbols that can be used to create a flowchart slide.

EnerGraphics enables you to draw freely on the screen. Corrections are easy to make using the special control keys offered by the software. EnerGraphics is also capable of creating arcs and curved lines on the drawing.

From the main menu, select the Two-Dimensional Graph option. This brings to the screen the Two-Dimensional Graph menu containing the options Symbol Design and Graphic Design. Select the first option, Symbol Design. EnerGraphics offers you two ways to draw a symbol on the screen. You can use a matrix design pattern like graph paper, referred to as *pixel-type design,* or you can produce the illustration "freehand" without the aid of the matrix. This is called *composite design.*

From the Symbol Design menu, select the Design option and hit the letter *A* to convert the screen from pixel to composite. In the center of the screen a plus sign will appear. The middle of the plus sign is where the line in your drawing will begin. To the right of the screen there is a list of control commands and the horizontal and vertical coordinates of the center of the plus sign.

Position the plus sign by moving the arrow keys. When the plus sign is in position, pressing the F1 function key will cause a line to be drawn when you move any of the arrow keys. To stop drawing, press the F1 function key again.

Once you have drawn the symbol, pressing the F9 function key will cause the menu to appear, enabling you to select the Save option. Save the symbol to disk. After your symbols are designed and stored on disk, they can be recalled and placed in position on the chart. By drawing your symbols ahead of time you can produce a flowchart in a few minutes by calling them up from the disk and placing them in the desired portion of the chart. When you have positioned all the symbols, the chart will be ready to be photographed.

We have discussed only some of the features that are available with EnerGraphics. With this software you can quickly produce complicated mechanical illustrations that can be incorporated into your slide presentation.

Using The Grafix Partner

In this chapter we have reviewed a number of useful business graphics software packages that make it easy for you to create presentation slides. Although these programs can be very helpful, there might be some situations when you don't want to leave your spreadsheet software and use such a business graphics package. For example, you may want to use Lotus 1-2-3, Symphony, or Framework. *The Grafix Partner* allows you to add dramatic graphics to Lotus 1-2-3 or enhance the graphics capabilities of both Symphony and Framework. The Grafix Partner will also work with other software like Lotus or as a stand-alone business graphics package.

The Grafix Partner is unique in that it can run concurrently with other software. You could load The Grafix Partner into your personal computer before Lotus 1-2-3 or virtually any other software that you are using. Unlike other programs, The Grafix Partner is designed to reside in the upper memory locations in your personal computer. Lotus 1-2-3 and similar programs are stored in a lower memory.

To activate The Grafix Partner, all you have to do is press the CTL, ALT, and plus sign keys simultaneously. The cursor will appear in the middle of the screen and look much like an enlarged plus sign. This is The Grafix Partner screen. The plus sign key on the numeric key pad is used to call up

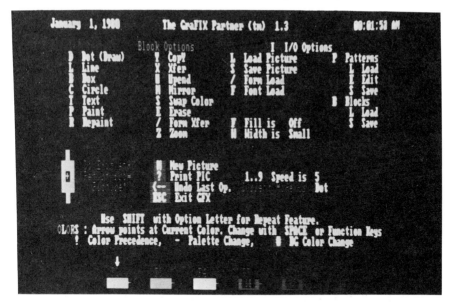

The Help menu of The Grafix Partner lists all of the options along with the key strokes necessary to activate each function.

The Grafix Partner's Help menu screen. The Help menu enables you to continue working with the program without referring to the instruction manual. The Help menu is also used to return you to the other program that is in the computer. Press the ESC key when this menu is on the screen, and the software will ask you to confirm your desire to leave The Grafix Partner. If you give a positive reply, the program will return to the original program you were working with. During the time The Grafix Partner is in use the operation of the other program is suspended.

Designing slides using The Grafix Partner is not difficult if you can supply the imagination. For example, if you want to draw a box on the screen, press the letter *B*. This places the program in the Box mode. Using the arrow keys, move the cursor to where you want the upper left corner of the box to be and press the space bar to lock the position in the software. Next, move the cursor to where you want the lower right corner of the box to be and press the space bar again to the lock this position. The software draws the box.

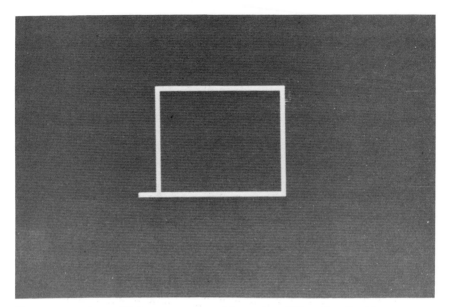

Even a novice will have no trouble using The Grafix Partner to create computer-generated illustrations. For example, suppose you wanted to remove the line that extends out of the box in this illustration.

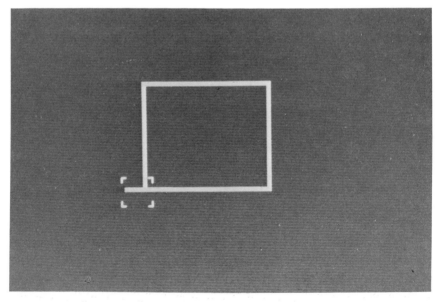

The line can be removed easily using The Grafix Partner's Zoom feature. Select this feature from the main menu, and a square cursor appears on the screen. Using the arrow keys, box in the area that you want to change.

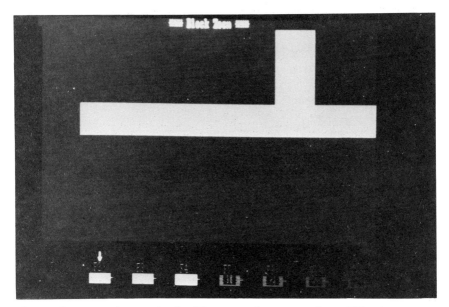

Once the area is marked off, press the space bar. The program zooms in to fill the screen with the boxed area of the illustration.

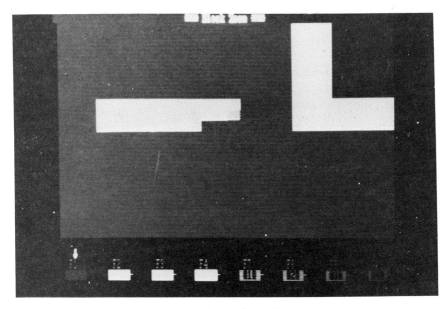

To remove the line, change the color of the cursor to match the background. By moving the cursor over the unwanted line, you can erase it.

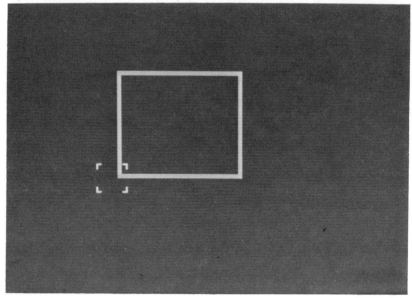

Press the ESC key to return to the full screen. As you can see, the line that extended out of the box has been erased.

Drawing circles is no problem for The Grafix Partner. Press the letter *C* to place the software in the Circle mode. Using the arrow keys, move the cursor where you want the center of the circle to be drawn and press the space bar. Move the cursor to the outside edge of the circle and press the space bar to lock in the position. The software draws the circle. If you are not pleased with the circle or the box, press the BACKSPACE key to remove the drawing from the screen.

You can add text to your slide with the Text mode by pressing the letter *T*. While in the Text mode you will have a choice of fonts, built into The Grafix Partner or you can purchase a font disk that will broaden your selection. Furthermore, The Grafix Partner has a font-generating program that enables you to create your own fonts. The characters that appear in the Text mode are *hollow,* or uncolored. Using the Paint mode of The Grafix Partner, you can color the text. Similar to other graphics software pack-

To draw a circle with The Grafix Partner, select the Circle mode from the Help menu. Establish the center of the circle by moving the cursor into position and pressing the space bar.

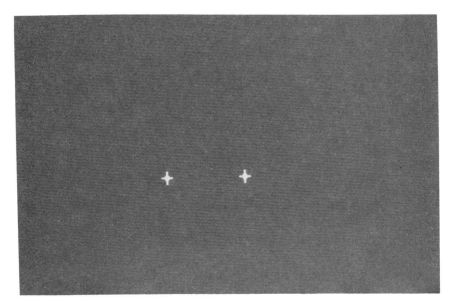

Once the center of the circle has been set, use the cursor to establish the diameter of the circle. Press the space bar to lock in the position.

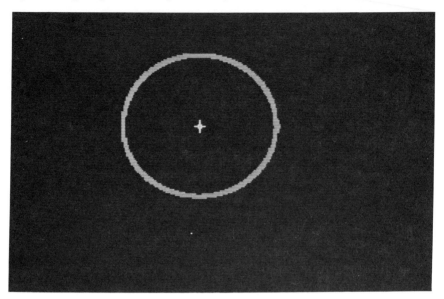

Press the space bar again, and the program will automatically draw a perfect circle. You can zoom in on a segment of the circle if you want to make any fine adjustments.

ages, The Grafix Partner offers several palettes of colors from which you can select.

The Grafix Partner offers some unique features that are useful when designing a slide for your presentation. For example, the software has a Block Copy option that allows you to copy an image on the screen to another portion of the screen. Suppose you designed a symbol that you want to use several times on the same slide. Instead of redrawing the symbol each time, you can have The Grafix Partner copy it. To do so, press the letter *Y* to enter the Block Copy mode. Using the arrow keys, move the cursor to the upper left corner of the image you want to copy and press the space bar. Move the cursor to the lower right corner and again press the space bar. This identifies the image that is to be copied. The image will be boxed on the screen. If some part of the symbol is not boxed, you can press the ESC key and reset the corners. If the boxed area is correct, press the space bar once more. Using the arrow keys, move the image to

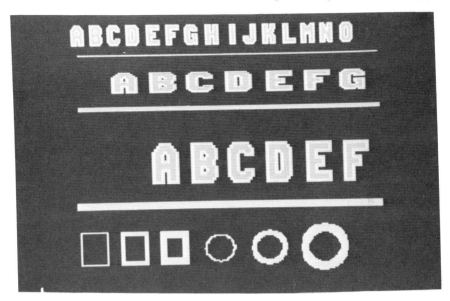

The Grafix Partner offers a wide selection of fonts. The letters shown here have been colored using the Paint mode. Notice that the program also enables you to use three different font sizes and line widths.

the new location. When you are satisfied with the position, pressing the space bar again fixes the copy of the image to the new position on the slide.

You can also transfer any image on the screen to a new location. Press the letter *X* for the Transfer mode and hit the space bar to establish the two opposite corners of the image area. The arrow keys are used to relocate the image and the space bar sets the image in its new position.

The Grafix Partner also has two unusual features that are fun to experiment with. These are the Upend and Mirror modes. Both modes are executed in the same way as the Copy and Transfer modes. The Upend mode turns the image you draw upside down, and the Mirror mode produces a mirror image of the boxed segment of the screen.

You can design your own slide on the screen of your personal computer with The Grafix Partner and later produce a printed copy of the slide. If your printer has the capabil-

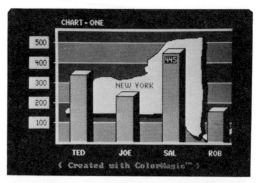

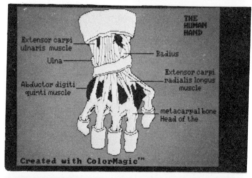

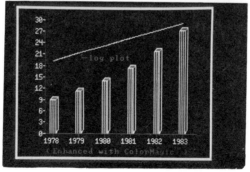

Created using ColorMagic, a version of The Grafix Partner.
Originals in full color.

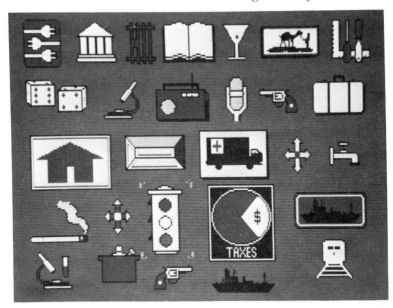

The Xfer mode of The Grafix Partner enables you to transfer an image from the program's illustration library to your slide. Here the traffic light symbol has been bracketed by cursors. By pressing the space bar you can move the symbol to your slide.

ity of printing in several colors, this software will print the image in color. This is an ideal feature for generating reproductions of your slides as part of the material that you hand out at the end of your presentation.

The Grafix Partner is an effective tool for creating presentation slides. Since The Grafix Partner resides in your computer along with your spreadsheet and word processing software, you can easily switch back and forth from program to program to verify data or review the text of your speech. You can see both your slide and your text and make changes without turning off your personal computer. The Grafix Partner is one of the few business graphics packages that offers this feature.

6

Using a Microcomputer as Part of Your Presentation

IN PREVIOUS chapters we have discussed how you can create presentation slides with your personal computer. You can also use your personal computer to display the slides during your presentation.

In some business situations, you will be called upon to speak before small groups in a conference room atmosphere. While a slide projector is still useful, it is cumbersome. Your personal computer can give better results than a slide projector in small-group situations. With special presentation software, your slides can be automatically presented on the screen of the computer in the sequence you select.

Practical Applications

Bringing a personal computer into a meeting can often be to your advantage. If you are a profit center manager, by having a personal computer nearby you can answer complicated questions posed by upper management in the middle of the meeting. For example, with the appropriate software you can graphically demonstrate the impact of various business conditions on your profit center. After changing a number or two in the program, you will have a full-color illustration of the new data. If a colleague needs to know how changes in the inflation rate will affect the outcome, again you only need to change a few numbers and the computer will show the results.

Like the profit center manager, financial executives who are seeking financing for their projects can use spreadsheet and business graphics software to generate almost any information that is requested.

Guidelines for a Computer Presentation

Although you can use the same images in your computer screen presentation that you used in your slide presentation, there are a few facts to consider before you design your show. You could employ the same business graphics software you used for the slide show, but there are two unique features that can be employed only in a computer screen presentation—computer animation and computer slide control.

When the term *computer animation* is mentioned, Hollywood-style computer special effects like those featured in the movie *Tron* come to mind. Personal computers and business graphics software have not reached the point, as of this writing, to duplicate the effects that are used in commercial film productions. However, they are sophisticated enough to give the illusion of motion on the screen. When used strategically during a computer presentation, even the crudest form of animation can give your presentation a real sense of drama.

For instance, you could create an animated sequence in which a pie chart is constructed slice by slice on the screen, showing your firm's marketing budget. As you discuss each expenditure, the corresponding slice of the pie could be positioned by the computer. Or you could use a bar chart to draw a graphic comparison between each division's budget. The individual bars could be programmed to grow or shrink to indicate the budgetary changes you are proposing. These simple effects are a sure-fire way to hold your audience's attention throughtout your presentation.

Still another application of computer animation you might consider is to use a map of the United States to illustrate the potential annual increase in sales that would result from the changes you propose. Instead of projecting this information on a standard bar chart, you could program the computer to represent each customer with a simple symbol. You could begin your presentation with the present number of customers on the map. Then, as your presentation progresses, the number of new customers projected by your research could pop up on the map. When your colleagues see old markets growing and new, previously untested markets appearing on the map, you can be certain that they will listen carefully to your proposal. Your carefully researched facts are the backbone of your presentation, but it never hurts to add some flashy graphics!

Unlike a slide projector, your computer can perform the job of changing the slides on its own. Once all of the images have been saved to a single floppy disk, you can program the business graphics software to recall each image to the screen in sequence, and you can designate the length of time the slide is to appear. If you choose not to follow a formal script, you can preselect the order of the slides and call them up to the screen by pressing a key on the keyboard. Similar to a slide projector, you can move ahead to a slide or return to a slide by pressing a single key.

Using a computer instead of a slide projector for a presentation to a small group has its advantages. For example, your slides cannot drop on the floor and become disorganized when they are contained on a floppy disk, and there is no need for a screen when the computer monitor is used to display the slides.

Lighting is sometimes a problem when using a slide projector. Since a computer monitor supplies its own light, the only difficulty you might run into is glare from the room lighting. This problem is easily overcome by turning off the room lights.

Some personal computers have detachable keyboards that enable you to place the computer monitor on a conference table, where everyone can see it, and still control the slides from a distance using the keyboard. With this feature you won't have to walk in front of the computer screen during the presentation.

The most important advantage a computer has over a slide projector is that the computer (especially the transportables) is self-contained. In many situations you will be able to set up the computer and begin your slide presentation within five minutes of entering the conference room. If you come properly prepared, you need only open the computer and plug it into an electrical outlet. When the computer is turned on, the business graphics program automatically loads into the computer and you are ready to give your talk. Remember, the best way to avoid annoying interruptions is to come prepared.

Which brings us to a potentially serious disadvantage of using a personal computer in place of a slide projector. The computer can distract the audience from the topic of the meeting. They may be so dazzled by the computer-generated slide show that they concentrate more on watching the computer producing the slides than on listening to the speaker. This best way to combat this problem is to make the purpose of the meeting and the information that is being presented more critical to the audience than their curiosity about the computer. You might also try beginning your presentation with a brief introduction to the computer, after which you can politely lead the audience directly into you presentation, reminding them that the information that will be discussed will be of great value to them.

To further reduce the distraction caused by the personal computer, you should use a computer monitor that can be separated from the computer itself. Ideally, the only computer hardware you should have on the conference table is the monitor. The computer keyboard and all other hardware should be situated out of the direct view of the audience but still be accessible to the speaker. Most transportable personal computers have built-in monitors. However, they can be upgraded to include a separate monitor port. With the computer and keyboard out of sight, the audience can concentrate on what the speaker is saying while they are looking at the images on the monitor.

If the audience consists of 15 or more executives, you should consider using more than one monitor. Cable adapters are available in computer or electronics stores to connect more than one monitor to the video output port of the computer. By strategically placing the monitors on stands at the corners of the room, you can be assured that everyone will have a clear, unobstructed view of the slides.

There are many business graphics software packages that have the capability of turning your personal computer into a slide projector. On the following pages we will take a close look at some of these programs. We will also explore how you can use business graphics software to create animation and put on a professional slide show.

Animating with ExecuVision

There are a variety of business graphics software packages that can create the illusion of movement on the computer screen. *ExecuVision* is one of these programs that has met with acceptance in the business community. In Chapter Five we discussed in detail how ExecuVision uses menus to help the user design slides. Since the same method is used in the animation segment of the program, you should review the ExecuVision section in that chapter.

The first thing to do when you are creating animation with ExecuVision is to create a base slide of the illustration you will be using (see Chapter Five). Once the slide has been created, save it to a floppy disk. This will enable you to load the design back into the computer if you accidently lose the image on the screen (i.e., from a power failure or by entering a wrong command). With your original slide always stored on disk, you are ready to create animation.

Earlier we mentioned an animated bar chart as a common application of computer animation in a business presentation. The essential idea is to have a moving bar chart visually demonstrate your proposal as you speak. To create this effect using ExecuVision, first create a version of your bar graph with the bar you intend to animate removed from the slide. This slide must be saved to a floppy disk.

☐ Return to the Create menu of the program, where you will find a submenu that contains the Motion option.

☐ Move the cursor to the word *Motion* and press the return arrow key. The Motion menu will appear on the screen. This function contains the following options: Move, Trail, Invert, Mix, and Exit. Select the Move option and press the return arrow key.

☐ After the Move option has been entered, the program will ask you to "scale and move the box to define pix." The program will animate everything contained within the box you define.

☐ Using the cursor control keys, move the box to the empty position on the bar graph. This should be at the baseline of the horizontal axis.

☐ When you have positioned the box, press the return arrow key. The computer will then ask you to "position the pix to destination."

☐ Using the up arrow key, move the cursor to the highest point on the bar graph. You have now given the program a destination for the bar. You still must determine its speed. How fast should the bar grow?

☐ If you want the bar to grow slowly, press the 1 key. This is the slowest speed.

☐ If you require a faster speed, you can press the key for any number from 1 through 9. The last number you press before pressing the return arrow key will be the speed selection used by the program during the animation.

☐ Press the return arrow key. The program will now automatically enter the Save Picture mode. You will be asked to enter the name of the slide.

☐ Enter the names and press the return arrow key. The slide containing the animation has now been saved to disk. You do not have to return to the Create menu to save the slide.

☐ To see the animation, load the slide back into the computer and run it during the Run Phase option selected from the main menu. This animated slide can now be incorporated into your computer-run slide presentation.

ExecuVision also has several more advanced animation capabilities that you can employ in your presentation. One of these is called the *trail technique.* The trail technique enables you to simulate a three-dimensional or layered look in your animation. For example, you could create an image of your product on a slide. The product is placed on the left side of the screen. Using the Trailing Motion option, you can spread the image of the product across the screen like a deck of cards being spread on a table. You see one complete image of the product laying on top of numerous other images whose edges appear on the screen. You might use this technique when you are discussing the number of variations within a product line. If your firm produces 10 variations of one product, for example, the slide can start with a full image of the first product and then spread across the screen showing one full image and nine edges.

If you really want to be creative using animation, then you should explore the *continuous-animation* feature of Execu-Vision. This feature enables you to create animation from slide to slide so that a motion appears continuous between slides. For example, for a very dramatic effect, you could have an airplane fly across the skyline of New York City. (ExecuVision's libraries provide you with a variety of professional-quality images that can be easily incorporated into your slide show.) For this effect you will need at least three slides, each a continuation of the city skyline. In each of the slides you incorporate the image of an airplane moving across the skyline, using the motion function of ExecuVision. Align the flight path of the plane so that it is the same in all the slides. ExecuVision has a feature called Ruler that helps you determine exact measurements between slides. When you run the slides in sequence, the plane will appear to fly from one slide to another. With your direction the program will make the end point of the motion of one slide the beginning point of the next slide.

It is important to understand that ExecuVision is not designed to produce sophisticated computer animation. You will not be able to produce a computer-animated cartoon show using this program. ExecuVision's animation feature is designed to give your slide show a "live action" feeling that adds a new dimension to graphic illustrations.

ASSEMBLING THE EXECUVISION SHOW

After creating various slides, it is important that a business graphics software package be able to assemble the slides and display them in sequence. ExecuVision has just such a feature, called Run Phase, that turns your personal computer into a slide projector.

- ☐ Select Run Phase from the main menu. This brings to the screen the Run menu that consists of the options Start, Entry, Auto, and Exit.
- ☐ Select the Entry option. The Entry option will bring to the screen the Prepare Table. This is a list of the saved slides that you have prepared.
- ☐ More the cursor to the name of the slide you would like to use as the first slide.
- ☐ Press the return arrow key to tell the computer to enter the Start option. This function enables you to view

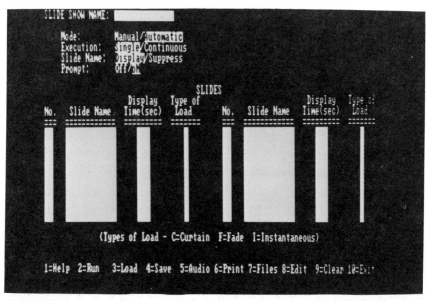

After you have created and saved all of your slides to disk, you can use the ExecuVision Slide Show menu to select the order of the slides and the length of time each will be shown.

each slide in the sequence you have set up on the Pre-pare Table, starting with the first slide that you se-lected.

☐ When the program is in the manual mode, you can control when the slides change by using the right ar-row key to advance to the next slide or the left arrow key to return to the previous slide The manual mode is essential when you want to stop during your com-puter slide presentation to answer questions from the audience. With it you can also easily return to any slide at any time during the meeting.

ExecuVision also has an automatic run feature that turns the process of displaying your slides over to the computer. From the Run menu, select the Auto option and press the return arrow key. The Auto menu appears on the screen with the following options: 4SEC, 8SEC, 15SEC, 30SEC, 1MIN, 2MIN, 4MIN, Exit. These are the run times for each slide. Select one of these times to determine the display time for each slide by moving the cursor to the desired time and pressing the return arrow key.

Although ExecuVision offers you a broad range of dis-play times (four seconds to four minutes), you should ex-periment using various selections for your presentation. Make your display time selection and then run the slide show as you read your script. It is beneficial to have a colleague in attendance to give you a feeling of working with an au-dience.

The Run menu will appear again when you have selected the display time, and the cursor will automatically be placed on the Start option. Press the return arrow key to begin the slide show. Although the program is on automatic display, ExecuVision does allow you to override this feature. At any time during the presentation you can hold a slide on dis-play longer by pressing the space bar. The slide will remain on the screen until the space bar is pressed again. The sec-ond time the space bar is pressed, the auto feature re-sumes. If you want to turn off the auto feature completely, press the ESC key. This will return you immediately to the Run menu.

If during your slide show it appears that the auto feature is not serving your needs and you don't want to return to the Run menu during the presentation, use the space bar to advance the slides. This uses the stop and run feature of the Auto option to momentarily halt the advancement of the slides. You have control over the advancement of the slide by activating this feature for each slide.

The Auto feature of ExecuVision has one drawback. The slide show will automatically recycle after the last slide is displayed. Press the space bar when your final slide is shown or ExecuVision will start your slide show over again.

Whether you use the manual mode to advance slides on your personal computer or use the automatic slide advancement feature, ExecuVision offers you the tools to use your personal computer as part of your presentation. You can create slides using your own art or with the many illustrations offered in the ExecuVision libraries. You can use still slides or incorporate animation using the program's motion feature. Then, for the final touch, you can select the sequence of the slides and have the program display them in order.

ExecuVision can be used for in-house meetings. When you combine ExecuVision with a transportable personal computer, the program is perfect for use during sales presentations to clients. As you become familiar with the various features of ExecuVision, you probably will not return to creating slides by hand.

Presenting with EnerGraphics

EnerGraphics is another business graphics software package that allows you to create a computer-generated slide show. Like ExecuVision, the EnerGraphics menu system was discussed in detail in Chapter Five, where we demonstrated the technique for designing a slide. You may want to review this aspect of the previous chapter before proceeding.

Although EnerGraphics does not offer the animation features that ExecuVision provides, EnerGraphics does enable you to rotate three-dimensional illustrations on the screen. If you don't need animation in your presentation, then consider EnerGraphics software.

The presentation feature of this program enables you to specify the order of the slides and to recall them in sequence during the meeting. When EnerGraphics loads, the main menu will appear on the screen. Select the Support option. The Support menu will appear listing three selections: Function Input, Convert Data Files, and Slide Presentation. You need the Slide Presention option.

The Slide Presentation selection brings another menu to the screen. This menu has the following options available: Create Control File, Verify Control File, Slide Presentation, Edit Control File, Save Control File, Read Control File, Delete a File, Show File Directory, and Return to the Main Menu.

Before you can begin to assemble your slide presentation, you must first have created several slides and saved those to a floppy disk. Chapter Five explains how to create slides using EnerGraphics. The following checklist goes through the steps in assembling the slides for a presentation.

☐ With the Slide Presentation menu displayed on the screen, select Create Control File by pressing the F1 function key. This brings up the control file form to the screen. A control file is the listing of the slides in order of appearance.

☐ The control file form asks you for the file name of the slide exactly the way it appears on the disk directory. You type in the name and press the return arrow key.

☐ Next the program asks you to select the color of the slide. A row of numbers appears near the bottom of the screen. Each number from 01 to 16 is a color code. The EnerGraphics manual references each code number to a color.

☐ Move the cursor key to the appropriate selection and then press the return arrow key.

☐ The program then needs to know the number of seconds that the slide is to appear on the screen. Type the number of seconds into the program at the prompt. If you do not want the program to display the slide automatically, type "zero." The program will allow you to advance the slide manually during the presentation.

☐ After you have completed filling in the data for the first slide, repeat the sequence for each one of the slides that will be used in the presentation. There is no problem if you make an error. You can press the F1 function key to insert a slide in the sequence or the F2 function key to delete a slide.

☐ When you have completed the control file form, press the CONTROL key and the END key at the same time. The program will then ask you for more information. It will prompt you for the name of the previous control file and the name of the next control file. Both of these prompts are used if you intend to run several sets of slides, each with its own control file. If this is the case, respond to the prompts with the names of the files. If you are not linking control files, press the return arrow key to advance the program.

☐ The Slide Presentation menu will then appear on the screen. The control file must now be saved to a floppy disk so it can be recalled when you are ready to give the presentation.

☐ Pressing the F5 function key followed by pressing the return arrow key will cause the control file form to appear on the screen again. The program then prompts you for the file name for the control file.

☐ Once you enter the name and press the return arrow

key, the program saves the control file to disk and returns the Slide Presentation menu to the screen.

☐ To be sure that all of the files are on the disk, press the F2 function key. This will have the program check the disk and verify that all of the files are present. The program will display the control file form and print, "All files were found."

☐ Once the files are verified, you can have the program run through the slide presentation. Press the F3 function key and the return arrow key and you are ready to begin the show.

☐ Press the plus sign key to bring the first slide to the screen. If you entered a time period on the control file form for the slide, the computer will automatically show the slide for that length of time and then advance to the next slide. If there was no time period indicated, you must press the plus sign key each time you want to advance the slide.

During the slide presentation you can hold a slide on the screen longer than its specified time period by pressing the space bar. To continue, you press the plus sign key. EnerGraphics also permits you to return to the previous slide by pressing the minus sign key.

EnerGraphics is an ideal program to use for presentations if your discussion will center around three-dimensional mechanical illustrations and flowcharts. The program is especially designed to create these illustrations as slides on your personal computer. Besides mechanical images, EnerGraphics can also produce two- and three-dimensional graphs from data.

Working without Special Software

Using a business graphics software package that has a manual or automatic slide presentation feature is convenient, but if this software is not available any business graphics or integrated software package can be used to create a similar effect. The presentation feature of a business graphics package only serves to recall files that contain the slide you have saved. This feature does make it easier and less time-consuming to bring the file to the screen than using other segments of the program (i.e., the load file function) to do the same thing. But the results are the same whether the load file function or the presentation feature is used—the slide is copied from the floppy disk and displayed on the computer screen.

If the software you are using does not offer the presentation feature, you can still use the graphics program for a presentation by using the load file function. Here are a few guidelines that will make it easier for you to present a smooth-running meeting.

Slides are usually saved to a floppy disk under a file name that describes the topic of the slide. For example, a slide indicating sales for 1986 might have the file name "SALES86." Long, descriptive file names are ideal when you aren't worried about the time it will take to recall the slide to the screen. But typing in a long file name during a presentation is time-consuming and can be distracting.

A more effective approach is to create and save the slides on a floppy disk as usual and then, after all of the slides have been saved, load and resave the slides to another floppy disk using abbreviated file names. This is a simple procedure. The original floppy disk containing the slides under their full file names is inserted into the disk drive. The slide that you will use in the presentation is then loaded into the computer. Remove the original floppy disk from the drive and insert the copy disk into the drive. The slide that is now contained in the computer is saved to the copy disk using the file name "A."

Repeat the same procedure loading the next slide for the presentation and saving it to the copy disk under the file name "B." During the presentation you will not have to be concerned about typing the full file names into the computer. Abbreviated file names reduce the amount of time it takes to activate the computer during a presentation. When the copy file disk is created, be sure that you prepare a list of the file names. The list should be kept handy for reference during the presentation. During the question and answer period after your presentation you will probably want to refer to some of the slides as you answer questions. Without a slide list or a slide presentation feature on the business graphics program, it will be very distracting if you have to search through the full series of slides for the proper illustration.

Although using a software package without a slide presentation feature does have its drawbacks, there are also some advantages. For example, if you use an integrated software package such as Framework, you have more capability at the meeting than if you had a presentation graphics software package. With Framework, you have a spreadsheet, database, business graphics, and more.

During a presentation involving a small audience, questions might be raised involving the projections used to create the business graph slides. For example, a colleague might want to know how a specific change would affect the outcome. With business graphics software, it would be difficult to show the effect of the change. However, with integrated software you can recall the model to the spreadsheet segment of the program and input the change as indicated by the colleague. The numerical results will immediately appear on the screen. You can easily use the same data and have the business graphics segment of the software produce a chart that illustrates the impact of the change. The use of an integrated software package in this manner will add depth and meaning to the presentation and leave the audience with an excellent impression.

With an integrated package it will take you more time to prepare the program for the presentation than if you were using a business graphics software package that contains a presentation feature. Besides having the the file names in an abbreviated format, you should also have the program that is to be used during the presentation cued to the first slide. Some business graphics and integrated software packages, for example, require you to sort through menus and submenus before the program is ready to accept the file name of the slide that is to be loaded. It is critical that this preparation be completed prior to the seating of the audience. When the audience is ready, you should begin the presentation immediately.

Another important technique you should incorporate into your presentation is to turn the monitor off after the computer and the program are ready for the meeting. Immediately before the meeting begins, have the computer call up the first slide. When the meeting is about to begin, the monitor is turned on and the first slide appears.

PFS FOR A PRESENTATION

One software package that can be used as part of a computer presentation is *PFS:Graph*. PFS:Graph, as discussed in detail in earlier chapters, is part of the PFS series of interactive programs that include PFS:Write, PFS:Report, and PFS:File. Although PFS:Graph is part of a series of software packages, this program can use data created with such spreadsheet software as VisiCalc or stand alone, enabling you to type data directly into the program. PFS:Graph is fully integrated with the other software packages in the PFS series.

There are two techniques you can employ when you use PFS:Graph as a presentation tool. You can either create the graph prior to the meeting and save it on a disk, or save the raw data to the disk and have the program create the graph during the meeting. Which technique you use for your presentation will depend on the nature of the subject you are discussing. For example, if a slide is designed to illustrate data that are not open to interpretation (i.e., last year's sales), then you should have the slide prepared in advance and saved on a disk. Data that are subject to interpretation (i.e., potential effects of market conditions on sales) should be saved in a raw format on disk. You should also consider preparing several sets of data using various assumptions about the influencing variables that affect market conditions. With this data quickly accessible from the disk during the meeting, you can respond positively to questions from the audience.

Working out the Details

PFS:Graph must be loaded into the computer prior to the beginning of the meeting. After the program is in memory, the computer will display the main menu, which lists the following options: Get/Edit Data, Display Chart, Define Chart, Save Chart, Get/Remove Chart, and Print/Plot. You will need the Get/Edit option.

☐ Press the number one followed by the CONTROL Key and the C key to bring the Get/Edit Data menu to the screen.

☐ This menu gives you three options: Enter/Edit Data, Get VisiCalc File, and Get PFS File. If you have not saved your graph to disk or if you intend to use a spreadsheet file, select Enter/Edit Data.

☐ Press the number one and then press the CONTROL key and the C key together to bring up the blank data form which is used to enter data from the keyboard. You can then enter the data following the prompt from the program.

☐ After the last item has been entered, press the CONTROL key and C.

☐ The program then checks all the values to make sure they are valid entries. If they are, it sorts the data and stores them in a working area of the program called the scratchpad. The program will return to the PFS Graph menu.

☐ You can select the Display Chart option by pressing first the number two, then the CONTROL key and the C key. This will bring the chart to the screen.

☐ With other functions available in PFS:Graph you can enhance the chart with titles. Once you have completed the chart, it can be saved to disk ready to be recalled during the meeting.

There will be occasions when you will use a spreadsheet file such as VisiCalc to enter data. When this is the case, select the second option from the PFS:Graph menu, Get VisiCalc File. When the data are loaded into PFS:Graph, you can manipulate the PFS:Graph program as if you had entered the data yourself using the keyboard.

Data files from a spreadsheet program must be prepared for use with PFS:Graph. Before you can store your spreadsheet file, you need to determine the portion of the spreadsheet that you want entered into PFS:Graph, and whether these data are contained in columns or rows. You should store only the data that you need so that PFS:Graph can read from the file as quickly as possible. Also, if you want to process the data by rows, you must save them by rows; and if you want to process them by columns, you must save them by columns. The manual that is supplied with your spreadsheet program will indicate the procedures for saving just the data that you require.

☐ Select the VisiCalc file and the computer will prompt you for the file name of the spreadsheet data and identification for the X and Y data.

☐ Identify this data by indicating the number of the row or column from the spreadsheet that will be used as the X and Y data for the chart.

☐ After you respond to the program prompts, it will copy the data from the spreadsheet data disk and load the information into the scratchpad segment of the program. The program then returns to the PFS:Graph menu.

☐ Now, select the second option, Display Chart. This will cause the program to display the graph.

☐ You can then use the various features of PFS:Graph to enhance the graph.

When you have finished fine-tuning the graph, you can save the graph to disk using the Save option on the main menu. During the meeting you can either use the graph you saved or load the data from the spreadsheet into PFS:Graph and create a new graph. If you have to answer a "what if" question, you can easily recall the data from the spreadsheet disk into the PFS:Graph. Once it is loaded, you can use the editing option from the main menu to view the data form containing the information. There you can alter the data accordingly then return to the main menu and have the program display the new graph. When you have all of the slides or data prepared, they should be saved to the same disk using the abbreviated file name technique.

MORE WITH FRAMEWORK

Framework is an integrated software package that is ideal for use during a presentation. Framework has, among other features, a spreadsheet and business graphics package built into the program. When Framework is loaded into your computer, all the features of the program are ready to use.

You can use this program to show the impact of various conditions on the outcome of a financial strategy. For example, the raw data used to develop the graph are input into the spreadsheet segment of the program prior to the meeting. You might have entered these data as part of the normal business routine. Once the data are entered, you should save this information to a floppy disk. During the meeting questions from the audience will usually dictate whether or not you will need the spreadsheet. If this situation does arise, the data can be quickly loaded into the spreadsheet. Once loaded, you can modify the data to answer any question.

With the new data entered into the spreadsheet, you can use a unique feature offered by Framework called the quick graph feature. This is primarily used to quickly convert the numeric data into an illustration. The objective of this feature is to present the illustration on the screen in a clear, simple form. You should not plan on enhancing the output from the quick graph feature; quick graph is not designed for that purpose.

Framework must know which of the columns or rows on the spreadsheet will be used for the graph. Framework requires a minimum of two adjacent spreadsheet cells. The F6 function key is used to highlight the cells that are to be used in the graph. By pressing the CONTROL key and the G key, the Graph menu will appear on the screen. (Framework was discussed in detail in previous chapters. You may want to return to those chapters to review the program's features and menus before proceeding.)

Among other options, the Graph menu has a selection to indicate whether your graph will have a column or row as its X-axis labels. The corresponding letter (C or R) is entered into the computer. Once this selection has been made, it is time go see the quick graph. Pressing the return arrow key will cause Framework to draw a bar graph of the data on the screen.

If a bar graph does not represent that data concisely, you can return to the Graph menu and select the Draw New Graph feature. From the Graph menu, a different selection of graph can be made, such as a line or marked points graph. Framework will then use the same spreadsheet data and illustrate them in the new form.

The quick graph feature is sufficient to handle those "on the spot" emergency situations during a presentation. However, using Framework spreadsheet and graphics features you can develop interesting slides. We have discussed various techniques for creating slides in a previous chapter. Once you have created slides, you can save them to a floppy disk. This is accomplished by selecting the Disk menu, which contains the Put Away option. After all of the illustrations have been saved, they are ready to be recalled to the screen during the presentation using the Disk menu.

When the meeting is about to begin, you should bring up the Disk menu and use the Get File By Name option to recall the slide to the screen. This technique is repeated until the presentation is completed. Besides graphic files, you can also recall other files such as database, word processing, and spreadsheet files. The situation of the presentation will dictate if you will require files other than graphic files.

Should You Use a Computer?

Reading about the techniques that you can employ when using a personal computer during a presentation raises the question of whether a computer should be used during your presentation. The response to this question will not be unanimous among executives. We have discussed both the attributes and the faults associated with the role of personal computers in presentations.

You must know your audience. Some members will find the use of a personal computer undesirable and a distraction from the focal point of the gathering. Other members will find this application of new technology a refreshing approach to the conventional method of communicating business ideas. Before deciding on the computer's role in the presentation, you should discuss the concept informally with a few colleagues. Informal discussions should also be held with some of the people you intend to invite. Their responses will help you reach a decision about incorporating the personal computer in the presentation.

Begin by using your computer as a reference tool during a small meeting with close colleagues. The computer could be used to recall a spreadsheet or database file to the screen to enhance the conversation. In the same type of setting, give a short presentation with no more than five slides using the computer. Then, when you are ready, use the computer for a full-scale conference table meeting.

Manufacturers of Business Graphics Hardware and Software for Personal Computers

Presentation Graphics Software Manufacturers

Accent Software, Inc.
3750 Wright Place
Palo Alto, CA 94306
The Graphic Solution (Apple)

American Computer Products, Inc.
7120 S.W. 48th Lane
Miami, FL 33155
Quickdraw (IBM)
Graphicstutor (IBM)

Animation Graphics
11317 Sunset Hills Road
Reston, VA 22090
Super Slide Show (Apple)

Apple Computer
20525 Mariani Ave.
Cupertino, CA 95014
MacPaint (Apple)

Ashton-Tate, Inc.
1015 West Jefferson Blvd.
Culver City, CA 90230
Framework (IBM)

Avant Garde Creations
P.O. Box 30160
Eugene, OR 97403
Ulra Plot (Apple)

Beagle Bros.
4315 Sierra Vista
San Diego, CA 92103
Frame-Up (Apple)

Brightbill Roberts & Co.
120 East Washington Street,
    Suite 421
Syracuse, NY 13202
The Grafix Partner (IBM)

Business and Professional Software
143 Binney Street
Cambridge, MA 02142
Screen Director (Apple)

Computer Station
11610 Page Service Drive
St Louis, MO 63141
Graphics Writer (Apple)

Comshare Target Software
1935 Cliff Valley Way
Atlanta, GA 30329
Image Maker (Apple)

Context Management Systems
23864 Hawthorne Blvd.
Torrance, CA 90505
Context MBA (IBM)

Decision Resources
21 Bridge Square
Westport, CT 06880
Chart Master (Apple, IBM)

Desktop Computer Software Inc.
Suite 29-303
303 Portrero Street
Santa Cruz, CA 95060
Graph 'N Calc (IBM)

Dickens Data Systems, Inc.
3050 Holcomb Bridge Road
Norcross, GA 30071
Wall Street Plotter (Apple)

Ferox Microsystems
1701 N. Fort Myer Drive
Arlington, VA 22209
Graphics Power (Apple, IBM)

Graphic Software Inc.
1872 Massachusetts Ave.
Cambridge, MA 02140
Super Chartman II (IBM)

Hypergraphics Corp.
807 West Hickory, Suite 202
Denton, TX 76205
Hypergraphics (IBM)

IMSI
633 Fifth Street
San Rafael, CA 94901
 4-Point Graphics (IBM)

Innovative Software
9300 W. 110th Street
Overland Park, KS 66210
 Fast Graphics (IBM)

Insoft, Inc.
P.O. Box 608
Beaverton, OR 97005
 Graforth (Apple, IBM)

Koala Technologies Corp.
4962 El Camino Real, Suite 125
Los Altos, CA 94022
 MicroIllustrator (Apple, IBM)

Lotus Development Corp.
161 1st Street
Cambridge, MA 02142
 Symphony (IBM)

Micrografix Inc.
1701 N. Greenville, Suite 703
Richardson, TX 75081
 PC Draw (IBM)

Peach Tree Software Co.
3445 Peachtree Road N.E.
Atlanta, GA 30326
 Peach Graphics (IBM)

Penguin Software
830 4th Ave.
Geneva, IL 60134
 Paper Graphics (Apple)

Prentice Hall, Inc.
200 Old Tappan Road
Old Tappan, NJ 07675
 ExecuVision (IBM)

Sensible Software Inc.
6619 Perhan Drive
West Bloomfield, MI 48033
 The Graphics Department (Apple)

Software Publishing Inc.
1901 Landings Drive
Mountain View, CA 94043
 PFS:series (Apple, IBM)

VisiCorp
2895 Zanker Road
San Jose, CA 95134
 VisiTrend/Plot (Apple, IBM)

Wadsworth Electronic Publishing Co.
Statler Office Building
20 Park Plaza
Boston, MA 02116
 Statpro (Apple, IBM)

Personal Computer Graphics Monitor Manufacturers

Amdek Corp.
2201 Lively Blvd.
Elk Grove Village, IL 60007

Amtron Corp.
2260 de la Cruz Blvd.
Santa Clara, CA 95050

Aydin Controls
414 Commerce Drive
Fort Washington, PA 19034

Conrac Corp.
600 North Rimsdale Ave.
Covina, CA 91722

Electrohome LTD
250 Wales Ave.
Tonawanda, NY 14150

Hitachi America
401 West Artesia Blvd.
Compton, CA 90220

Leading Edge Products Inc.
225 Turnpike Street
Canton, MA 02021

Micro Display System Inc.
1310 Vermillion Street
Hastings, MN 55033

NEC Home Electronics
1401 Estes Ave.
Elk Grove Village, IL 60007

Princeton Graphic Systems
1101-I State Road
Princeton, NJ 08540

Quadram Corp.
4357 Park Drive
Norcross, GA 30093

Sakata USA
651 Bonnie Lane
Elk Grove Village, IL 60007

Sanyo Electronics Inc.
1200 West Artesia Blvd.
Compton, CA 90220

Sony
Sony Drive
Park Ridge, NJ 07656

Taxan (TSK Electronics)
18005 Cortney Ct.
City of Industry, CA 91748

USI Computer Products Div.
150 North Hill Drive
Brisbane, CA 94005

Zenith Data System
1000 Milwaukee Ave.
Glenview, IL 60025

Manufactures of Hard-Copy Hardware
Plotters

Alpha Merics Corp.
20931 Nordhoff Street
Chatsworth, CA 91311

Amdek Corp.
2201 Lively Blvd.
Elk Grove Village, IL 60007

Apple Computer Inc.
20525 Mariani Ave.
Cupertino, CA 95014

Cal Comp.
2411 West La Palma Ave.
Anaheim, CA 92803

Comrex International
3701 Skypark Drive
Torrance, CA 90505

Enter Computer
6867 Nancy Ridge Drive
San Diego, CA 92121

Hewlett Packard
974 E. Arques Ave.
Sunnyvale, CA 94088

Houston Instrument
8500 Cameron Road
Austin, TX 78753

Panasonic of America
One Panasonic Way
Secacus, NJ 07094

Radio Shack
1400 One Tandy Center
Fort Worth, TX 76102

Roland DG
7200 Dominion Circle
Los Angeles, CA 90040

Strobe, Inc.
897-5A Independence Ave.
Mountain View, CA 94043

Electrosensitive Printers

Apple Computer Inc.
20525 Mariani Ave.
Cupertino, CA 95014

Axiom Corp.
1014 Griswold Ave.
San Fernando, CA 91340

Impact Dot Matrix with Graphics

Anacom General
1116 East Valencia Drive
Fullerton, CA 92631

Anadex, Inc.
9825 De Soto Ave.
Chatsworth, CA 91311

Apple Computer
20525 Mariani Ave.
Cupertino, CA 95014

Axiom Corp.
1014 Griswold Ave.
San Fernando, CA 91340

Cannon USA
One Cannon Plaza
Lake Success, NY 11042

Centronics Data
1 Wall Street
Hudson, NH 03051

C. Itoh
5301 Beethoven Street
Los Angeles, CA 90066

Data Impact Products
745 Atlantic Ave.
Boston, MA 02111

Dataproducrs Corp.
6200 Canoga Ave.
Woodland Hills, CA 91365

Datasouth
4216 Stuart Andrew Blvd.
Charlotte, NC 28210

Digital Equipment Corp.
146 Main Street
Maynard, MA 01754

Dynax Inc.
5698 Bandini Blvd.
Bell, CA 90201

Epson America
3415 Kashiwa Street
Torrance, CA 90505

Facit Inc.
235 Main Dunstable Road
Nashua, NH 03061

Genicom
One General Electric Drive
Waynesboro, VA 22980

Hewlett Packard
974 E. Arques Ave.
Sunnyvale, CA 94088

Hi-G Printers Corp.
101 Locust Street
Hartford, CT 06114

IBM Corp.
P.O. Box 1328
Boca Raton, FL 33432

Infoscribe Inc.
2720 South Croddy Way
Santa Ana, CA 92704

Lear Siegler, Inc.
714 North Brookhurst Street
Anaheim, CA 92803

Mannesmann Tally
8301 S. 180th Street
Kent, WA 98032

Micro Peripherals, Inc.
4426 South Century Drive
Salt Lake City, UT 84123

Mindware Inc.
15 Tech Circle
Natick, MA 01760

NEC Home Electronics
1401 Estes Ave.
Elk Grove Village, IL 60007

North Atlantic/Quantex
60 Plant Ave.
Hauppauge, NY 11788

Okidata
532 Fellowship Road
Mt. Laurel, NJ 08054

Panasonic of America
One Panasonic Way
Secaucus, NJ 07094

Personal Micro Computers
475 Ellis Street
Mountain View, CA 94043

Printek
1517 Townline Road
Benton Harbor, MI 49022

Printronix, Inc.
17500 Cartwright Road
Irvine, CA 92713

Radio Shack
1400 One Tandy Center
Fort Worth, TX 76102

Start Micronics, Inc.
888 Washington Street
Suite 311
Dedham, MA 02026

Texas Instruments
P.O. Box 402430
Dallas, TX 75240

Toshiba America, Inc.
2441 Michelle Drive
Tustin, CA 92680

Transtar
P.O. Box C-96975
Bellevue, WA 98009

Trilog, Inc.
17391 Murphy Ave.
Irvine, CA 92714

Ink Jet Printers

Advanced Color Technology
21 Alpha Road
Chelmsford, MA 01824

Canon USA
One Canon Plaza
Lake Success, NY 11042

Diablo
901 Page Ave.
Fremont, CA 94537

Docutel/Olivetti
106 Decker
Irving, TX 75206

Ope Printers, Inc.
505 White Plains Road
Tarrytown, NY 10591

PrintaColor Corp.
5965 Peachtree Corners East
Norcross, GA 30071

Quadram Corp.
4355 International Blvd.
Norcross, GA 30093

Sharp Electronics Corp.
10 Sharp Plaza
Paramus, NJ 07652

Siemens Communications
5500 Broken Sound Blvd.
Boca Raton, FL 33431

Radio Shack
1400 One Tandy Center
Fort Worth, TX 76102

Laser Printers

Canon USA
One Canon Plaza
Lake Success, NY 11042

Thermal Printers

Alphacom
2323 South Bascom Ave.
Campbell, CA 95008

Axiom Corp.
1014 Griswold Ave.
San Fernando, CA 91340

Trendcom/3M
480 Oakmead Pkwy.
Sunnyvale, CA 94086

Thermal-Transfer Printers

Toshiba America
2441 Michelle Drive
Tustin, CA 92680

Photographic Image Makers

Celtic Technology
6265 Variel Ave.
Woodland Hills, CA 91367

Dunn Instruments
544 Second Street
San Francisco, CA 94107

Eastman Kodak Co.
343 State Street
Rochester, NY 14650

Image Resources
2260 Townsgate Road
Westlake Village, CA 91361

Lang Systems, Inc.
1010 O'Brien Drive
Menlo Park, CA 94025

Matrix Instruments
230 Pegasus Ave.
Northvale, NJ 07647

Modgraph Inc.
1393 Main Street
Waltham, MA 02154

Polaroid Corp.
575 Technology Square
Cambridge, MA 02139

Manufacturers of Color Graphics Boards

Amdek Corp.
2201 Lively Blvd.
Elk Grove Village, IL 60007

Applied Data Systems
9811 Mallard Drive
Laurel, MD 20708

Control Systems
2855 Anthony Lane
Minneapolis, MN 55418

Discortex Corp.
87 Bethpage Road
Hicksville, NY 11801

Eagle Computer Inc.
983 University Ave.
Los Gatos, CA 95030

Frontier Technologies Corp.
P.O. Box 11238
Milwaukee, WI 53211

Hercules Computer Technology
2550 Ninth Street
Berkeley, CA 94710

IDEAssociates Inc.
7 Oak Park Drive
Bedford, MA 01730

Imaging Technology Inc.
600 W. Cummings Park
Woburn, MA 01801

Matrivision, Inc.
26 Beacon Street
Burlington, MA 01803

Micromax
6868 Nancy Ridge Drive
San Diego, CA 92121

Paradise Systems, Inc.
150 N. Hill Drive
Brisbane, CA 94005

Plantronics Enhanced Graphics
  Products
1751 McCarthy Blvd.
Milpitas, CA 95035

Quadram Corp.
4355 International Blvd.
Norcross, GA 30093

Scion Corp.
12310 Pinecrest Road
Reston, VA 22091

Sigma Designs, Inc.
2990 Scott Blvd.
Santa Clara, CA 95050

STB Systems, Inc.
601 N. Glenville Ave.
Richardson, TX 75081

Tecmar
6225 Cochran Road
Solon, OH 44139

Index